WTF R U Sayin'?

Codes, Acronyms, Abbreviations, and
Phrases: The shorthand of the digital age

By Mitch Sexton

ISBN: **1535370297**

ISBN-13: **978-1535370295**

DEDICATION and ACKNOWLEDGMENTS

This is dedicated to my wife, Sue, and to my family, all of whom have provided an unending supply of love, support, and encouragement.

To all those, including a host of anonymous contributors on the internet, who put up with my constant inquiries and contributed to the construction of this collection. They have freely provided their feedback and encouragement. It is my belief that if everyone had the support of (known and unknown) friends like these we would live in a much better world.

Table of Contents

What is this book?

It is a dictionary (of sorts) modeled after the first English dictionary. If you will hang in there with me, you will see the connection.

By the end of the 1500's, England had to deal with an explosion of new words entering the language due to developments in literature, science, medicine, and the arts, as well as a renewed interest in classical languages.

In 1604, to help people understand and use this new information, English schoolmaster Robert Cawdrey published *Table Alphabeticall*. It was the first single-language English dictionary.

Previously, books of this type were bi-lingual—for example, English to French, Spanish to English—offerings. Cawdrey's book listed about 3,000 words, along with a simple, brief description of each one and, occasionally, a demonstration of how to use the term.

Because of the public's limited education, Cawdrey's efforts provided a much-needed book that would identify both the spelling and the definition of each term. He intended his work to be "useful for any unskillful persons."

Nearly 150 years later, Samuel Johnson followed Cawdrey's lead and published *A Dictionary of the English Language*.

Enter the digital age

The prose of modern day correspondence is divided between formal and informal language.

Formal language is the writing style you learned in school and you use it for letters, contracts, magazines, newspapers, books, etc.

The informal language of the digital age is different from the official language taught in schools. Informal language—the spoken word—is the everyday language, good-natured or bad, and includes slang as used by people at work and play. In its digital form, as used across social media, informal messages are generally in lower case and punctuation is almost non-existent.

For special occasions, to emphasize an idea, or to express an emotion, the sender may type some terms in all capitals. However, keep in mind the only rule in informal messaging is that writing your entire message using all caps is considered shouting; and shouting is considered rude!

If you have not already guessed, I should warn you that some of the language falls into the area of *street vernacular*—the language of the streets—and may offend readers because it can be crude, blunt, rude, and even vulgar.

Whether participants are in their homes, among friends, or in groups, you will find their messages cram emails, text, and the other social network venues.

Today, while the average person knows many more words than their forebears, their informal day-to-day working vocabulary averages less than 5,000 words. This provides an efficient reduction in words, but the digital age created a greater need for short-form codes, acronyms, and abbreviations. The goal of this generation's user is to create a message that communicates the crux of an idea without being bogged down by a lot of fluff. Twitter, with its current 140-character limit, is a shining example of the opportunity to communicate using fewer characters.

Caution should be exercised as a message could be reduced from intelligence to garbage, if such coding is overdone. However, when done right, use of these shortcuts makes the job of communicating—whether texting via your cell phone, or through any of the other forms of social media—more efficient. This push for speed and efficiency caused many of the niceties of prior communication forms, such as grammar and punctuation, to fall by the wayside.

Would I be offended?

Because some of the terms fall into the area of street vernacular, you can see that this is not a book for elementary school kids.

While you may consider street language crude, rude, vulgar, and in poor taste and could be offended by its use, this document attempts to list a collection of terms and their definitions in order that you can better understand what is said and, more importantly, what you might be saying. In other words, are you saying what you think you are saying?

As an example, there is an abundance of acronyms involving the ever-popular *F-bomb*, (words such as fuck and some of its many associated variations: f**k, f***, f------ , fark, feck, ferk, flak, fork, frak, frap, freak, frick, frig, futz, fudge) frequently appear on the list. An urban legend, one of many, is that the acronym has its roots in 15th century England and is alleged as an abbreviation for the then legal term *For Unlawful Carnal Knowledge*. While the legend is colorful and tinged with a type of historical romanticism, it is not true. More probable, the word (defined as "to strike") stems from an earlier period and was injected into the English language from any number of its previous invading contributors. Possibly candidates are Roman/Latin, Low German, Frisian, Norse, Scottish, or Dutch.

 Depending on your point of view, some argue that with many of these terms, the acronyms used would work just as well without the added expletives. The other school of thought seems to be that adding expletives convey not only the meaning, but also the emotions of the message. Use and non-use are the sender's choice. In some cases, although it probably obvious, I listed some versions with and without the expletive to show that you have a choice.

In some definitions, I have made use of a version of various "don't care" symbols (for example *, $, or - giving: f**k, F------, A$$ or *a*) where I figured that translation was obvious.

How did all of these terms evolve you ask?

Anthropologists claim that previous communications efforts have become part of the folklore passed on in a manner similar to oral traditions.

That might be good to know, but what methods are used to create terms? I can think of a few ways.

Some terms, as BYOB (Bring Your Own Booze), are created by using the first letter of each word. A similar method would be to use the first letter of major words, ignoring articles such as A/AN or THE, the in order to produce a more compact acronym.

Individuals, driven by "the need for speed" have sometimes made their own terms by dropping most vowels and some consonants from a word or phrase in order to turn THANKS into TKS.

Alternately, some terms may be derived phonetically using word sounds. For example, words like THANKS may become THX. C is sometimes substituted for 'See', while U may be substituted for 'You', or R for 'ARE'. Jeep received its name because people phonetically slurred the initials of the words used to identify the military's *General-Purpose* vehicle.

Some police/fire codes used on popular TV programs provide an abundance of terms, which have inserted themselves into the language. In a similar manner, but to a lesser extent, you will see some CB and amateur radio terms, emoticons, along with acronyms originally used by foreign participants. Users, familiar with older technologies, move up to the new technologies but carry the terminology they are comfortable with, along with them.

Some terms have been around for ages. It is rumored that BFE (Butt F**king Egypt) probably dates back to when Caesars' Legions first invaded that county. Scanning the list, you see terms like, SNAFU (Situation Normal, All Fouled Up), BYOB (Bring Your Own Booze), OTL (Out to Lunch), RE (Regarding), and others sprinkled throughout.

This happens because a group adopts a particular method of communicating and members share their knowledge with others within the group. Nothing remains static. Words and phrases once popular soon lose their luster as new terms come along. As terms spread, these codes morph into multiple definitions depending on the group, and the subculture within a group, and they get a life of their own. Each group has an explanation and justification for their variation in method and tradition.

Understandably, groups may claim supremacy and each maintain the belief that they are correct in the application and use of the methods, the acronym, and its meaning. This works as long as all parties to the message agree on the same definition. Take the acronym BAM. Depending on the group, it might mean *Below Average Mentality* while in another group it might mean *Bust A Move*.

Similarly, different codes might be used to communicate the same message. CD9 and POS both are variations of *Parent over Shoulder*, along with more than a dozen other codes.

This reinforces the concept that some terms stem from oral tradition, our environment, our vocation, our region. Because of this, you will find many close variations of the same term. However, one way or another, these terms have been absorbed and passed around through the digital culture where members have applied them as they saw fit making it a chaotic situation as far as what and how a term is used.

Common Abbreviations:

The collection I included is by no means complete as it is ever evolving and may never be complete. To get this list, I polled social media and sifted through materials submitted by users in response to my requests.

Because of these wide-ranging origins, the list includes deviations in the acronym (the same acronyms with a different definition; conversely, the same definition may be associated with different acronyms). I believe these differences may be due to cultural, regional, or vocational attributes.

Depending on your background, your region, or the context of your message, a term may have different meanings.

Understandably, you may not agree with my selections, but please keep in mind that we do not all talk with the same jargon, accent, or tone. As you proceed, you will find that not everyone uses the same codes in the same way.

While not suitable for formal business correspondence, these abbreviations add flavor and speed up typing in personal and informal conversations. What is amazing is the depth of digital vocabulary that has been built.

The two lists, Alphabetical by Code and Alphabetical by Description, follow. Look them over and see for yourself ....

Codes, Acronyms, Abbreviations, and Phrases: The shorthand of the digital age (Alphabetical by Code)

Symbol Codes	Descriptions
!	I have a comment
""""8*#"	Drunk
#	Hashtag/Pound Sign/Number Sign used in Twitter to make it easier to find messages with a specific theme
#BEMYGUEST	A hashtag letting others know you'd like to exchange guest blog posts
&&	And
&&&&	Pretzels
(( )):**	Hugs and kisses
(::()::)	Band aide
(_)	Drinking glass
****	Popcorn

poof	Goodbye
*<[:{)	Santa
G	Giggle
S	Smile
W	Wink
....	Speechless
---/--@	Rose
:'	Crying
:-#	Lips are sealed
:-&	Tongue tied
:(	Frown
:'-(	Crying sadly
:-(	Sad
:( )	Can't stop talking
:)	Smiling face
:'-)	Crying with joy
:-)	Smile
:-)	Smile
:-)*(-:	Kiss
:*)	Clowning
:*)	Drunk
:@	Angry and swearing
:-@	Screaming
:-\	Undecided
:-{}	Blowing a kiss
:{}::	Sneezing
:-|	Ambivalent
:~/	Mixed up
:->*<-:	French kiss
:-6	Exhausted - Wiped out
:-9	Delicious/Yummy
:C	Really sad

:-C	Bummed out
:-C	Unbelievable
:D	Big smile
:-i	Indifferent
:O	Surprised
:-O	Mouth open in surprise
:-P	Sticking out tongue
;-)	Wink
;0	Surprised
;S	Gentle warning like "Hmm? What did you say?"
?	Huh?
?	I don't understand what you mean
?	I have a question
?	What?
?4U	I have a question for you
?DUM?	What do you mean?
?RUD	What are you doing?
@	At
@--)--)(--	Rose
@[ ]~~	Mug of hot coffee or tea
@REPLY	A Twitter update directed as a reply
@TEOTD	At The End Of The Day
[X]	No spam!!
_/	Glass (drink)
_/7	Cup (coffee/tea)
\~/	Full glass
\M/	Heavy Metal Music
\-O	Bored

^^	Means "Read Line above"
^^	means "Read Message above"
^5	High five
^URS	Up yours
__/__	Applause
|*-*|	Cassette tape
|c|	Can of coke
|-i	Asleep
|-O	Yawning
|p|	Can of Pepsi
~~!!~~	No joke?
<>	Clap
<3	Heart
<33	Heart or love (more 3s indicate bigger heart)
<3u	Love you
<CHUCKLE>	The sender chuckles
<EG>	Evil Grin
<FROWN>	The sender is frowning
<G>	Grin
<GRRR>	I'm so angry
<SMILE>	The sender is smiling
<SMIRK>	The sender is smirking
<WINK>	The sender is winking
=)	Smile
> :-(	Devilish
> > :-(	Angry
> ><<*>	Fish/fishy
>:@	Really angry and swearing

>;->	Devilish wink
0.02	My (or your) two cents worth
000	Airhead
000	Time
0001000	I'm feeling mighty alone right now
0001000	I'm feeling mighty alone/left out right now!
001	Please
007	I've got a secret
010	I'm Tired
010	Plans changed
011	Monday
0121	I'm Confused
020202	Just thinking of you
022	Tuesday
024	I'm heading to the beach
033	Wednesday
044	Thursday
05-05	Margaritas dude! (Cinco de Mayo)
055	Friday
064	Don't Call Me
066	Saturday
07	Just kidding
074	I Need A Favor
077	Sunday
07734	Hello
080808	Hugs and Kisses
099	I've got something stupid to tell you

099	Too Late To Call
1	You the man!
1	You the one!
1	You're the one!
1	You da man!
10	Your perfect
10	You're perfect
10000001	I miss you
1001	Prove It
100-2-1	The odds are against you
101	Come home by (time)
101	I've got an easy question
10-1	Bad reception
10-1	Emergency
10-1	What Is Correct Time
10-20	What is your location
10-20	Where are you?
10-2-1	It's possible; there's a chance
10-2-1	slim chance
1023	It's Over
103	Call
10-33	Emergency - All stations stand by
1-0351123-400	I want you
10-38	Correct time
104	Everything's O.K.
10-4	Everything's O.K.
10-4	Is everything OK?
1040	You owe me big time
10-400	Thank you

105	Cancel that
106	Change
107	Return here
108	Come Over
108	Deliver to
109	You forgot
10-9	Say again
10M	Ten man (online gaming)
10Q	Thank you
10qs	Thanks
10sion	Tension
10X	Thanks
11	Maybe
11	Skiing/Snowboarding (This suggests a set of skis)
1-1	Thank you
110	Go to
111	Help
11111111	Congratulations!
112	Going now
113	Lost
114	Meet
116	Negative /No
118	In reference to
119	I'm in trouble
119	Rescheduled - Change to
120	Not available
1200	Want to have Lunch?
121	I need to talk to you alone

121	One-to-one (private chat initiation)
121	Wait
121212	Happy Birthday
122	I want you
122	Will get in/Will Arrive at
1225	Merry Christmas
12-25	Merry Christmas
123	I Miss You
124	Affirmative/Yes
124	I'm dreaming of you
125	I'm bored
1250	Me Too
12C4	Un de Ces Quartre/One of these days
13	I'm having a bad day
13-30	I'm having a bad day and it's getting old
1337	Elite
135	You Wish
13579	This is odd
14	Hi
14	Hi*
141	I'm with you
143	I Love You
143	I love you
1432	I love you too
1432222222	I love you so much
1443	I don't love you
1492	Let's go sailing
14AA41	One for all and all for one
15	Whatever

15243	Be With Me
1543	I Still Love You
17	No
1701	Live long and prosper
1776	Your revolting
1776	You're revolting
18	Yes
1-8	I ate
1-8	I ate
180	Yesterday
1-800	I'm free
182	I hate you
183	I'm busy
187	You're Dead
19	Zero hand (online gaming)
1925	Let's go out
193	Miss Me?
195	See you tonight
197	I'm pissed off
1CE	Once
1DR	I wonder
1NAM	One in a million
1TG	Number of items needed for win (online gaming)
1UP	Extra life (online gaming)
2	To
20	Location
200	Near a phone
200	Tonight
2001	Your way out there
2001	You're way out there

202	I can't meet you
203	Hang up the phone
205	Item is completed
206	Item is not completed
207	Get together with me
209	In route
21	Let's have a drink
210	No answer
211	Come get me
212	I'll get you
213	I've taken care of it
214	Got your message
215	Will be late
216	In a traffic jam
217	Thanks
218	Not going to wait any longer
219	Car problems
22	Be Good
2-2	Now we dance
2-2	Now we dance; shall we dance?
220	Why haven't you called?
221	Where are you?
222	Busted
222	Pick me up after school
222	Pick me up after school
22222222	Going to sleep
224	2-Good-4-U
23	Te Amo/I Love You (Spanish)
2357	Primed (Lists all prime

	numbers under 10)
24	I'm Home
24-24-24	Go for a Beer?
243	We love you
244	My Sexy Baby
2468	You're terrific
247	24/7 (All day - every day!)
25	Sorry
25252525	Hugs and Kisses
26	Te Quiero/I Love You (Spanish)
265	Check your mail
27	Need you
280	My Sexy Baby
288	Today
29	You Suck
2-9T	Tonight
2B	To be
2C4SKOOL	To cool for school
2C4U	To cool for you
2CUL	To cool
2CUTE	Too cute
2D4	To die for
2DAY	Today
2EZ	Too easy
2F	Too Funny
2F4U	Too Fast For You
2FF	Too F**king Funny
2G2BT	Too good to be true
2l8	Too late
2M2H	Too much to handle

2MI	Too much information
2MOR	Tomorrow
2MORO	Tomorrow
2MORROW	Tomorrow
2MRW	Tomorrow
2NTE	Tonight
2TG	Number of items needed for win (online gaming)
2U2	To You Too
2W	Two Wheeler (motorcycle)
30	This is getting old
300	Airport
301	Park
302	Bank
303	Daycare
303	Stop Playing
304	Hoe
304	House of worship
305	Drycleaners
306	Meeting Group
307	Night Club
308	Doctors Office
309	Friend's Place
310	Supermarket
311	Fitness Center
312	Home
313	Hospital
314	At the job site
315	But
316	Meeting or Appointment
317	Theatre

318	At my place
319	At my work
32	Eat Me
321	Please reply
321	Social Gathering
322	At the place we talked about
323	Family member's house
324	See you soon
324	Service Center/Garage
325	Restaurant
326	School/University
327	Shopping Center
328	Sports Game
329	Music Store
333	What's up?
341	I Like You
343	Call back now
346	Call Back Please
350	I'm sorry for you-know-what
36	Your cool
360	I love you back
365	I'm blowing you a kiss
38	(ET) Phone Home
385	Hi Cutie / handsome
390	Best of luck to you today
395	Please be careful out there!
4	For
4	Want to play golf?
400	Want to hear something

	stupid
404	Car/ Truck
404	I don't know
404	Karma(what goes around comes round)
4040	I Hate You
405	I've got a secret
406	Hugs & kisses
406	Hugs and Kisses
41	Call Me
410	You owe me big time
411	I Need Information
411	I need some information
419	keys
42	F**k You
420	Got weed?
420	Let's get high
420	Marijuana
420	Who pulled your chain?
420	You're in trouble buddy
423	Call Me Now
425	Call Me Later
426	Call me tonight
428	Call me tomorrow
428	Call me whenever
428	Tickets
429	Video
43	F**k You
430	You did it! Bravo!
434	Feel Better
435	Are we having fun yet?
436	Hugs and Kisses

440	Cheer up!
444	I want Love
445	Ditto to your last page
45	Good night
45	Goodnight
455	Don't make me come get you
45-56	Good night - Sweet dreams
459	I love you (ILY is 459 on phone keypad)
46	Hug
46	Just Kidding
460	Mind your own business
465	Don't be lolly-gagging around
47	Good morning
470	I'm with you thru thick & thin
477	Best friends forever
480	What goes around comes around
485	A quick howdy to you!
49	Good afternoon
490	You're in loony land
495	Go for it!
4AO	For adults only
4COL	For Crying Out Loud
4EAE	Forever and ever
4EVA	Forever
4EVR	Forever
4FN	For fun

4GET	Forget
4NR	Foreigner
4U2C	For you to see
4va	Forever
4W	Four Wheeler (standard van or auto)
4YEO	For your eyes only
5	Hi
5-0	Are you booked?
5-0	Let's go to Hawaii
5012124	Sorry
5050	Maybe
50-50	It doesn't matter to me; what do you want to do?
50-50	Maybe
511	Too much information (more than 411)
52	Hurry up
522	Think Of Me
53	Thank You
54	Never mind
54321	I'm on my way
54321	I'm ready to explode
55	Let's cruise
555	Sobbing/crying (Mandarin Chinese)
55555	Crying your eyes out (Mandarin Chinese)
55555	Laughing (In Thai language '5' is pronounced 'ha')
56	Sweet dreams

56	Sweet dreams
58	Happy Birthday
59	Fine
5900	I feel sick
59173	Hugs
5N	Fine
6	Always
600	Adjust your attitude
601	Happy Birthday/Anniversary
603	Hope you're feeling better
605	Don't leave
606	Bitch
607	I miss you
609	I'm mad at you
610	I'm scared
611	I'm sorry
612	I'm thinking about you
613	It's late - Get home!
614	Just wanted to say Hi
616	Stay away for a while
617	Stop calling me
618	I'm not going to Beep you again
619	Wish you were here
621	You are the greatest!
637	Always & forever
66	I'm mad
66	Lets hit the road
6771	Good Friend
69	Lets get together

69999	Get In Line
6Y	Sexy
7	Forever
70	I'm sad
707	Laughs Out Loud
710	I'm out of gas
710	I'm out of gas (Read upside down)
73	End of Message
747	Let's fly
7735	Sell out
7K	Sick
8	Ate
8.O	Shocked and surprised
800	Boo
8-084-804	B-day-boy
81	Hells Angels (H=8th letter; A=1st letter of alphabet)
811	Not an emergency - but very important!
82	Freak Me Out
823	Thinking of you
831	I love you (8 letters - 3 words - 1 meaning)
8383	Bebe
8484	Ha Ha
86	Over
86	You Are Finished
86	You're finished
8642	I'm gonna get even with you

87	I'm late (Read upside down)
87	Late (meant to be read upside down)
87	You're late (Read upside down)
88	Bye-bye (Mandarin Chinese)
88	Hugs and kisses
883	Page/text me now
8O	Shocked
9	Parent is watching
90	Beautiful
90*90*90	No! No! No!
90210	I'm feeling kinda wicked
911	Emergency
911	This is an emergency - Call me now!
92134-1111	I'm here
93	Grow up
937	Never
943	Where Are You
9-5	It's quitting time
98-6	Hope you're feeling better
99	Good morning
99	Nighty-night
99-44-100	I'm almost completely (99 & 44/100%) bored
9T	Night

A Codes	
A	Hey
A/N	Author's note
A/S/L	Age/sex/location
A2	Adios/Goodbye
A2D	Agree To Disagree
A2T	Addicted To Texting
A3	Anytime - Anywhere - Anyplace
AA	Alcoholics Anonymous
AA	As above
AA	Ask about
AAF	Always And Forever
AAF	As a friend
AAF	As a matter of fact
AAK	Alive and kicking
AAK	Asleep At Keyboard
AAMOF	As A Matter Of Fact
AAMOI	As A Matter Of Interest
AAP	Always A Pleasure
AAR	At any rate
AARDVARK	A Kenworth T-600 (nicknamed 'the anteater')
AAS	Alive and smiling
AATK	Always At The Keyboard
AAYF	As always - your friend
ABBR	Abbreviation
ABC	Already been chewed
ABD	Already been done
ABFWOT	A Big F**king Waste Of Time

ABT	About
ABT2	About To
ABTA	Good-bye (signoff)
ABU	All buggered up
ABWOT	A Big Waste Of Time
AC	Acceptable content
ACC	Anyone can come
ACD	ALT+CONTROL+DELETE
ACDNT	Accident
ACE	Important CB'er
ACE	Marijuana
ACF	Another Cluster F**k
ACK	Acknowledge
ACORNP	A Completely Obsessive Really Nutty Person
ACPT	Accept
ACQSTN	Acquisition
AD	Active Duty
AD	Adios
AD	Adult Disease
AD	All Day
AD	Anno Domini (Year of Our Lord)
AD	Associate Degree
AD	Associate Director
ADA	Adios Amigo
ADAD	Another Day Another Dollar
ADBB	All done - bye-bye
ADD	Address
ADDY	Address

ADIH	Another Day In Hell
ADIP	Another Day In Paradise
ADL	All Day Long
ADMIN	Administrator
ADMINR	Administrator (Government)
ADN	Any Day Now
ADPIC	Always Dependable (but) Politically Incorrect
ADR	Address
ADVENTURITTER	An adventurous Twitterer
ADVERTISING	A police car with its lights on
AE	Area effect (online gaming)
AEAP	As early as possible
AF	Aggression factor (online gaming)
AF	April Fools
AF	As *Freak*
AF	As If
AF	Audio Frequency
AFAIAA	As far as I am aware
AFAIAC	As Far As I Am Concerned
AFAICT	As Far As I Can Tell
AFAIK	As Far as I Know
AFAIR	As Far As I Remember
AFAIUI	As far as I understand it
AFAP	As Fast As Possible
AFAYK	As Far As You Know
AFC	Away from computer

AFD	All F**king Day
AFDN	Any F**king Day Now
AFFA	Angels Forever - Forever Angels
AFGO	Another F**king Growth Opportunity
AFJ	April Fools Joke
AFK	Away from Keyboard
AFN	All For Now
AFPOE	A fresh pair of eyes
AFT	About F**king Time
AFTER BURNER	Linear Amp
AFU	All F**ked Up
AFWW	Anyway For What It's Worth
AFZ	Acronym Free Zone
AGI	Agility (online gaming)
AGL	Angel
AGO	Another Growth Opportunity
AH	A$$Hat - Somebody with the head so far up their a$$ they could use it as a hat
AH	At Home
AHFY	Always Here For You
AI	Artificial Intelligence
AIAMU	And I am a money's uncle
AIGHT	Alright
AIH	As It Happens
AIMP	Always In My Prayers

AIP	Agreement In Principle
AIR	As I remember
AISB	As I Said Before
AISB	As It Should Be
AISI	As I See It
AITR	Adult in the room
AIUI	As I Understand It
AKA	Also Known As
AKI	Here
ALAMO CITY	San Antonio Texas
ALAP	As Long As Possible
ALCON	All concerned
ALERT	Affiliated League of Emergency Radio Teams
ALL THE GOOD NUMBERS	Best wishes
ALLIGATOR RADIO	CBer who is "ALL Mouth and NO Ears"
ALLIGATOR SKINS	Tread parts from a blown 18 wheeler tire left on the road
ALLIGATOR STATION	Tire shop
ALOL	Actually Laughing Out Loud
ALR	All Right
ALT	A Lot
AMAICR	As Much As I Can Recall
AMAIR	As Much as I Recall
AMAP	As much as possible
AMAZN	Amazing

AMBW	All my best wishes
AML	All My Love
AMOF	As a matter of fact
AMS	Ask Me Something
AN1	Anyone
ANCIENT MARINER	Someone who uses AM
ANFAWFOS	And Now For A Word From Our Sponsor
ANFSCD	And Now For Something Completely Different
ANKLE BITER	Small child or annoying teenager
ANL	Automatic noise limiter
ANTENNA FARM	Base station with many antennas strung up in the air
ANTLER ALLEY	Deer Crossing
ANTM	America's Next Top Model
AO	Anarchy Online (online gaming)
AOC	Available On Cell
AOE	Area of effect (online game)
AOL	Administrators On-Line (may be monitoring)
AOL	America On Line
A-OLs	Administrators On-Line
AOM	Age of majority
AOM	Age of Mythology (online gaming)
AOMM	Always On My Mind

AOS	Administrator Over Shoulder
AOTA	All of the above
AOYP	Angel on your pillow
APAC	All praise and credit
APB	All Points Bulletin
APP	Application
APPLE	A CB addict
APPLIANCE OPERATOR	Non technical person who just knows how to turn the rig on
APR	Appreciate
AQAP	As quick (or quiet) as possible
ARC	Archive (compressed files)
ARE	Acronym rich environment
ARG	Argument
ARITF	A Ripple In The Force
AS	Another Subject
ASAFP	As Soon As F**king Possible
ASAP	As Soon As Possible
ASAT	As Simple As That
ASAYGT	As Soon As You Get This
ASIAS	Gracias/Thanks
ASIG	And so it goes
ASL	Age - Sex - Location
ASLA	Age - Sex - Location - Availability
ASLP	Age - Sex - Location -

	Photo
ASMOF	As A Matter Of Fact
ASTRODOME CITY	Houston Texas
ASTRONAUT	A Police plane or helicopter
AT	About Time
ATB	All The Best
ATEOTD	At the end of the day
ATM	At this moment
ATSITS	All the stars in the sky
ATSL	Along The Same Line
ATT	All The Time
ATTWACTION	Describes an attraction between two users
ATTWICTED	Describes someone who is addicted to Twitter
ATW	All The Way
ATYS	Any Thing You Say
AUJ	Aujourd'hui/Today
AV	Antivirus
AVID	Audio Visual
AWA	As Well As
AWC	After while crocodile
AWESO	Awesome
AWGTHTGTTA	Are We Going To Have To Go Through This Again?
AWHFY	Are We Having Fun Yet?
AWOL	Absent With Out Leave
AWT	At What Time
AWTTW	A Word To The Wise

AWTY	Are We There Yet
AYBABTU	All your base are belong to us (online gaming)
AYDY	Are you done yet?
AYEC	At your earliest convenience
AYFKM	Are You F**king Kidding Me?
AYFS	Are You F**king Serious
AYK	As You Know
AYKM	Are You Kidding Me?
AYOR	At Your Own Risk
AYS	Are You Serious
AYSOS	Are you stupid or something?
AYT	Are you there?
AYT	At your terminal
AYTMTB	And You're Telling Me This Because
AYV	Are you vertical?
AYW	As You Were
AYW	As You Wish
AYWK	As You Well Know
AZM	Awesome
AZN	Asian
B Codes	
B	Back
B	Be
B TOWN	Birmingham Alabama
B&	Banned

B&M	Bacon and Mushrooms
B&M	Bitching and Moaning
B&M	Brick and Mortar
B&W	Black and white
B/C	Because
B/F	Boyfriend
B/G	Background (personal information request)
B/L	Buddy List
B1SUR	Bien Sur/Of Course
B2B	Business-to-business
B2C	Business-to-consumer
B2K	Back to keyboard
B2W	Back to work
B4	Before
B4N	Before now
B4N	Bye For Now
B8	Bait (person being teased)
B8	Bait (under-aged person as in 'jail bait')
B9	Boss is watching
BA	Bad A$$
Baby Bear	Rookie Cop
BAC	Back To Computer
BAC	Bad A$$ Chick
Back 'em Up	Slow Down
BACK DOOR	Behind you or to the rear
BACK DOOR CLOSED	Rear Of Convoy Covered From Police
BACK OFF THE HAMMER	Slow Down

BACK OUT	Driver Has Finished Talking
BACK OUT	I have finished talking
BACK'EM UP	Slow down
BAD SCENE	A crowded channel
BAE	Babe or baby
BAE	Before anyone else
BAFO	Best and final offer
BAG	Busting a gut
BAK	Back At Keyboard
BAL	Boite aux lettres/Mailbox
BALLET DANCER	An antenna that really sways
BAM	Below Average Mentality
BAM	Bust A Move
BAMF	Bad A$$ Mother F**ker
BAO	Be aware of
BAR CITY	Forrest City Arkansas
BAREFOOT	Using An Unmodified CB
BAS	Big A$$' Smile
BAS	Big 'butt' smile
BASE STATION	Radio At A Fixed Location
BASOR	Breathing a Sigh Of Relief
BAT	Bad A$$ Trick
BAU	Business as usual
BAY	Back at ya
BAY CITY	San Francisco CA
BB	baby
BB	Be back
BB	Bebe/Baby

BB	Bebi/Baby (Spanish)
BB	Big Brother
BB	Bye Bye
BBB	Boring Beyond Belief
BBB	Bye Bye Baby
BBC	Big bad challenge
BBERRYTWEET	A Tweet send from a Blackberry device
BBFN	Bye Bye For Now
BBIAB	Be Back in a Bit
BBIAF	Be Back In A Few
BBIAM	Be Back In A Minute
BBIAS	Be back in a sec
BBL	Be Back Later
BBM	Brains By Mattel
BBML	Be Back Much Later
BBN	Bye-bye now
BBR	Burnt Beyond Repair
BBS	Be Back Shortly
BBT	Be Back Tomorrow
BBW	Be Back Whenever
BBW	Big Beautiful Women
BBW	Big Black Women
BC	Be cool
BC	Because
BCAS	Because
BCC	Blind courtesy copy
BCNU	Be Seeing You
BCO	Big Crush On
BCOS	Because
BCOY	Big crush on you
BCOZ	because

BCP	Beaucoup/A lot
BCUZ	Because
BD	Big Deal
BDAY	Birthday
B-DAY	Birthday
BDN	Big darn number
BDU	Brain Dead User
BE BOP	Radio control signals
BEAM	Directional Antenna
BEAN BOPPER	Pill head
BEAN HOUSE BULL	Trucker talk exchanged at truck stops eyeball-to-eyeball
BEAN POPPER	Pill Popper
BEAN TOWN	Boston MA
BEAR	Police Officer
BEAR BAIT	Speeding car
BEAR CAGE	Police station or jail
BEAR CAVE	Police Station
BEAR IN THE AIR	Police In Helicopter
BEAR IN THE GRASS	A speed trap
BEAR TAKING PICTURES	Police with radar
BEAR TRAP	Stationary Police W/Radar
BEARFOOT	Using an unmodified CB transmitter
BEAST	A CB rig
BEAT THE BUSHES	To drive ahead of the others and try to lure out the police

BEAVER	Female
BEAVER BAIT	Money
BEAVER BEAR	Female Cop
BEAVER PALACE	Nightclub/Singles bar
BEAVER PATROL	On the hunt for a women
BEAVER TRAP	Sharp looking rig with custom interior
BEER BUST	Party
BEER CITY	Milwaukee WI
BEER TONE	An intermittent tone signal
BEER TOWN	Milwaukee WI
BEETWEET	A hot tweet - usually a popular trending topic on Twitter
BEG	Big Evil Grin
BELF	Blood Elf (online gaming)
BETTER HALF	Significant Other/Spouse
BF	Best friend
BF	Black Friday
BF	Boy Friend
BF	Brain Fart
BF2	Battlefield 2 (online gaming)
BFAW	Best friend at work
BFB	Big F**king bitch
BFD	Big F**king Deal
BFD	Big Freakin' Deal
BFD	Big Frickin Deal
BFE	Butt F**king Egypt
BFF	Best Friends Forever
BFF4LIFE	Best friend forever for life

BFFAE	Best friend(s) forever and ever
BFFF	Best F**king Friends Forever
BFFL	Best Friends For Life
BFFLNMW	Best friends for life no matter what
BFFN	Best friend for now
BFG	Big F**king Gun
BFG	Big Friendly Giant
BFG	Big freaking grin
BFI	Big F**king Idiot
BFN	Bye For Now
BFR	Big Freakin' Rock
BFS	Bull F**king S**t
BFU	Brain Free User
BFU	Butt F**king Ugly
BG	Big Grin
BGD	Background - A request for more information
BGF	Best Guy Friend
BGR	Boy-Girl Relationship
BGWM	Be gentle with me
BH	Better Half
BH	Bloody Hell
BH@	Be Home At
BHD	Behind
BHL8	Be Home Late
BHS	Be Home Soon
BI	Big Idiot
BI	Bi-sexual
BIB	Boss is back

BIBO	Beer in - Beer out
BIC	Butt In Chair
BIF	Before I Forget
BIG A	Amarillo TX
BIG APPLE	New York NY
BIG BEAR	A full blown bear (state trooper)
BIG CHARLIE	FCC
BIG D	Dallas TX
BIG DADDY	The FCC
BIG DOG	Police car with a radar detector
BIG HOLE	Top Gear
BIG M	Memphis TN
BIG MACK	Mack Truck
BIG MAMA	9 foot whip antenna
BIG R	Roadway Express Truck
BIG RIG	An 18 Wheeler
BIG RIG	Fancy expensive CB radio
BIG ROAD	Interstate
BIG SLAB	Expressway / Freeway
BIG T	Tucson AZ
BIG TRUCK	An 18 wheeler
BIH	Burn in hell
BIKINI STATE	Florida
BIL	Brother-In-Law
BIO	Bathroom break
BION	Believe it or not
BIOYA	Blow It Out Your A$$
BIOYN	Blow it out your nose
BIRD DOG	Radar Detector

BIRD-OF-MOUTH	Using Twitter to circulate news and information
BIS	Best in slot (online gaming)
BISLY	But I Still Love You
BIT ON THE BRITCHES	Got tagged for a speeding ticket
BITMT	But in the meantime
BITS	Back In The Saddle
BJ	Blow Job/Blowjob: A sex act
BK	Back
BK	Be Kool
BK	Because
BKA	Best known as
BL	Belly laugh
BL	Buddy List
BLACK'N WHITE	Cop
BLACK'N WHITE CBER	Cop with CB in his car
BLEEDING/BLEED OVER	Interference from a station on another channel
BLESSED EVENT	A new CB rig
BLEW MY DOORS OFF	A loud or strong signal
BLEW MY DOORS OFF	Passed With Great Speed
BLNT	Better luck next time
BLOODY	Frequently used English slang expletive
BLOWING SMOKE	Exaggerating - Telling of tall tails

BLTN	Better Late Than Never
BLUE SLIP	Ticket
BM	Bite Me
BM&Y	Between me and you
BMBO	Blow My Brains Out
BME	Based on my experience
BMIC	Boy Am I Confused
BN	Bad News
BND	Banned
BNI	Batteries Not Included
BNIB	Bad News In Box
BNO	Boys' Night Out
BNR	But Not Really
BNSCD	But now something completely different
BO	Back Off
BOAST TOASTIE	A self-proclaimed CB expert
BOAT ANCHOR	An old radio that is unrepairable
BOB	Back off *buddy*
BOB TAIL	A cab with no trailer attached
BOBFOC	Body Off Baywatch - Face Off Crime watch
BOBTAIL	Driving Tractor With NO Trailer Attached
BOC	But of course
BOC	Butt On Chair
BODACIOUS	Awesome
BOE	Bind on equip (online gaming)

BOGO	Buy One - Get One (free or at discount)
BOHICA	Bend Over Here It Comes Again
BOL	Be On Later
BOLO	Be on the look out
BOM	Buddy of mine
BOME	Based On My Experience
BOOMS	Bored Out Of My Skull
BOOTLEGGER	Running illegal station
BOP	Bind on pickup (online gaming)
BOS	Boss Over Shoulder
BOS	Brat Over Shoulder
BOSMKL	Bending over smacking my knee laughing
BOT	Back On Topic
BOT	Beyond that
BOT	Robot
BOTB	Back Of The Book
BOTD	Benefit Of The Doubt
BOUT	About
BOX	Tractor Trailer or Linear Amplifier
BOY SCOUTS	The State Police
BOYDS	Back Off You Dipstick
BOYF	Boyfriend
BPLM	Big person little mind
BQ	Bonus Question
BR	Bathroom
BR	Best Regards

BR	Big Road (major highway)
BRAKE CHECK	Traffic Is Slowing Ahead - Possibly To A Stop
BRB	Bath Room Break
BRB	Be Right Back
BRBB	Be right back *babe*
BRD	Bored
BREAK/BREAKER	Request use of a busy channel
BRH	Be right here
Bright Lights	Kansas City KS
BRING IT BACK	Answer back
BRING YOURSELF ON IN	Request to move into the right lane
BRNC	Be right back - nature calls
BROWN PAPER BAG	Unmarked Police car
BRS	Back real soon
BRS	Big Red Switch
BRT	Be right there
BRUSH YOUR TEETH AND COMB YOUR HAIR	Radar trap ahead
BS	Be Safe
BS	Bulls**t
BSC	Basic
BSF	But seriously folks
BSOD	Blue Screen Of Death
BSS	Besitos/Kisses
BSTD	Busted

BSTS	Better Safe Than Sorry
BSU	Better shut up
BT	Between technologies
BT	Bite this
BTA	But Then Again
BTAIM	Be That As It May
BTB	By The By
BTDT	Been There - Done That
BTFW	By The F**king Way
BTHO	Back The H*LL Off
BTHOOM	Beats The Hell Out Of Me
BTK	Back to keyboard
BTO	Big Time Operator
BTOBD	Be There Or Be Dead
BTOBS	Be There Or Be Square
BTSOOM	Beats the Sh*t Out Of Me
BTT	Back to topic
BTW	Between
BTW	By The Way
BTWITIAILWU	By the way I think I am in love with you
BTWN	Between
BTYCL	Booty call
BU	Butt Ugly
BUAI	Between You And I
BUBBA	A not-so-formal name for a good neighbor
BUBBLE GUM MACHINE	Police car with flashing lights on top
BUBHYE	Bye Bye

BUBI	Bye Bye
BUBU	Slang term for the most beautiful of women
BUCKET MOUTH	Loud mouth - or Someone who uses a lot of profanity
BUCKET OF BOLTS	Eighteen wheeler
BUCKEYE STATE	Ohio
BUG OUT	To leave a channel
BULL CITY	Durham NC
BULLDOG	Mack Truck
BULLTWITT	Fake false or over embellished Tweets
BUMPER LANE	Passing lane
BUMPER STICKER	Car Too Close To Bumper
BUTTON PUSHER	A third-party CBer trying to breakup communication between two other stations by keying his microphone or playing sounds
BW	Be Well
BWBR	Blonde With Brunette Roots
BWG	Big Wide Grin
BWL	Bursting With Laughter
BWQ	Buzz Word Quotient
BWTM	But Wait There's More
BYCA	Before you came along
BYE	Response to BYE?
BYE?	Are you ready to say

	goodbye?
BYF	Before You Forget
BYG	Be my guest
BYGWL	Busting my gut with laughter
BYKT	But You Knew That
BYOB	Be your own boss
BYOB	Bring your own beer
BYOB	Bring Your Own Booze
BYOB	Bring Your Own Bottle
BYOC	Bring your own computer
BYOD	Bring your own device
BYOH	Bat you on (the) head
BYOM	Bring Your Own Mac
BYOP	Bring your own paint (paintball)
BYTM	Better You Than Me
BZ	Busy
C Codes	
C	See
C&G	Chuckle & grin
C&P	Copy and Paste
C/P	Cross post
c2c	Care to chat
C4N	Ciao For Now
CAC	Cool As A Cucumber
CAD	Control + Alt + Delete
CAD	Short for Canada/Canadian
CADET	Can't Add - Doesn't Even

	Try
CAM	Camara/Camera
CARE BEAR	Police car located within a construction zone
CASH REGISTER	Toll Booth
CATCH YA ON THE FLIP FLOP	See Ya On Return Trip
CB	Chat break
CB	Coffee break
CB	Crazy Bastard
CB	Crazy Bitch
CBB	Can't Be Bothered
CBFB	Can't Be F**king Bothered
CBI	Come back later
CBS	Come back soon
CC	Courtesy copy
CD9	Code 9 - Parents or Supervisor around
CDO	Cuando/When
CELEBRITY SYNDROME	When a non-celebrity Twittter user believes they are a celebrity
CFAS	Care for a secret?
CFB	Check Face Book
CFN	Cell phone
CFU	Completely F**king Useless
CFV	Call For Votes
CFW	Can't F**king Wait
CFY	Calling for you
CH	Come here

CHICKEN COUP	Weigh Station
CHICKEN LIGHTS	Extra Lights On A Truck
CHINGO	Chat Lingo
CHIX	Chicks
CHK	Check
CHOO-CHOO	Chattanooga TN
CHX	Chicks
CIAO	Good-bye (Italian)
CICO	Coffee in - Coffee out
CICU	Can I See You
CID	Consider It Done
CID	Crying In Disgrace
CIGAR CITY	Tampa FL
CITY KITTY	City Police
CK	Sick
CKBK	Click back
CLAB	Crying like a baby
CLD	Could
CLEAN SHOT	Road Is Clear Of Police Ahead
CLK	Click
CLU	Cool like you
CM	Call me
CMAP	Cover my *a* partner (online gaming)
CMB	Call Me Back
CME	Checking My email
CME	See Me
CMIIW	Correct Me If I'm Wrong
CML	Call me later
CMM	Change(d) my mind
CMON	Come on

CN	Can
CNP	Continued Next Post
CO	Conference or Company
COA	Course Of Action
COB	Close of Business
COC	Code Of Conduct
COD	Call Of Duty
COH	City of Heroes (online gaming)
COL	Crying Out Loud
COMEDIAN	Center Median Strip
COMIC BOOK	Trucker's Log Book
COMIN IN LOUD & PROUD	Strong CB Signal
COMP	Computer
CONESTOGA	Flatbed trailer with ribs and soft top
CONV	Conversation
CONVO	Conversation
COS	cause (Because)
CO-TWITTERER	A second person on a single Twitter account
COUNTY MOUNTY	Sheriff
COVERED WAGON	Flatbed Truck With Sides And A Top Cover
COZ	Because
CP	Cell phone
CP	Chat post (or continue in IM)
CPE	Coolest Person Ever
CPP	C Plus Plus
CR	Chat room

CR8	Create
CRA CRA	Slang term for crazy
CRAFT	Can't remember a freaking thing
CRANK TWEET	A misleading tweet similar to a crank phone call
CRB	Come right back
CRBT	Crying really big tears
CRE8	Create
CRIT	Critical hit (online gaming)
CROTCH ROCKET	Motorcycle
CRS	Can't Remember S**t
CRS	Can't remember stuff
CRTA	Can't Remember The Acronym
CRZ	Crazy
CS	Cause
CSG	Chuckle/Snicker/Grin
CSL	Can't stop laughing
CSS	Counter-Strike Source (online gaming)
CT	Can't talk
CTC	Call The Cell
CTC	Care to chat
CTC	Cut the crap
CTFU	Cracking the F**k Up
CTHU	Cracking the *heck* up
CTN	Can't Talk Now
CTN	Can't Talk Now
CTO	Check This Out

CTP	Cutie pie
CTR	Center
CTS	Change the subject
CU	Completely useless
CU	See You
CU2	See You Too
CUA	See you around
CUIAL	See you in another life
CUL	Catch You Later
CUL	Cool
CUL	See you later
CUL8R	Catch You Later
CUL8R	See you later
CULA	See you later alligator
CUMID	See you in my dreams
CUNT	See You Next Time (Originally used in Morse Code but is seldom used due to its derogatory implications)
CURLO	See you around like a donut
CUS	See You Soon
CUT	See you too
CUTTL	Crawling under the table laughing
CUTTWEET	Refers to a retweet that is a shortened version of the original
CUZ	(be)Cause
CUZ	Cousin
CUZO	Cousin

CUZSIN	Cousin
CW	Can't Wait
CWD	Chat Word Dictionary
CWFL	Can't win for losing
CWOT	Complete Waste Of Time
CWYL	Chat With You Later
CX	Correction
CY	See YA
CYA	Cover Your A$$
CYA	See Ya
CYAL8R	See You All Later
CYE	Check your e-mail
CYEP	Close your eyes partner (online gaming)
CYL	Call you later
CYL8R	See you later
CYM	Change your mind
CYM	Check your email
CYO	See you online
CYOA	Cover Your Own A$$
CYOTFS	Catch Ya On The Flip Side
CYS	Check your settings
D Codes	
D/CED	Disconnected
D/L	Download
D/LD	Downloaded
D/LG	Downloading
d-_-b	Listening to music
D00D	Dude

D100	Descends/Get down
D2	Dedos/Fingers (Spanish)
D46?	Down for sex?
D8	Date
DA	Dumb A$$
DA	Yes (Russian)
DAC	D'accord/OK
DAC	Duck And Cover
DAH	Dumb A$$ Hole
DAILY TWITAMIN	A tweet that contains useful knowledge sent out daily
DAIZ	Days
DAL	Dumb a** loser
DAOC	Dark Age of Camelot (online gaming)
DAQ	Dumb A$$ Question
DAT	That
DATZ	That's
DAU	Doesn't Add Up
DB4	Day Be Fore (before)
DBA	Doing business as
DBEYR	Don't believe everything you read
DBG	Don't Be Gay
DBMN	Don't Bug Me Now
DC	Disconnect
DC	Don't Care
DC	Don't come
DCED	Disconnected
DD	Dear (or Darling) daughter

DD	Due diligence
DDG	Drop dead gorgeous
DDM	Don't disturb me
DDSS	Different Day - Same Sh**
DDSS	Different Day - Same Stuff
DEADHEAD	Drive An Empty Truck and Trailer To Get A Load Elsewhere
DED	Dead
DEETS	A shortened version of details
DEEZ NUTZ	A phrase used in online chat to annoy those involved
DEFGT	Don't even f**king go there
DEGT	Dear (or Darling) daughter
DEGT	Don't even go there
DERBY CITY	Louisville KY
DERP	Stupid or silly
DETWEET	Describe a tweet made then deleted
DEW	Adios/Goodbye
DFC	Don't F**king Care
DFCL	Dificil/Difficult
DFH	Dirty F**king Hippy
DFKDFC	Don't F**king Know Don't F**king Care
DFKM	Don't F**king Kill Me
DFL	Dead *freaking* last

	(online gaming)
DFL	Dead F**king Last
DFR	Dirty F**king Redneck
DFTBA	Don't Forget To Be Awesome
DGA	Don't go anywhere
DGAC	Don't give a care
DGAF	Don't give a *freak*
DGT	Don't go there
DGTG	Don't go there girlfriend
DGTMF	Don't go there my friend
DH	Darling Husband (usually used with a hint of sarcasm)
DH	Dirty Hippy
DH	Dumb Hippy
DHAC	Don't Have A Clue
DHAFC	Don't Have A F**king Clue
DHU	Dinosaur hugs (used to show support)
DHYB	Don't Hold Your Breath
DIAF	Die in a fire
DIESEL COP	D.O.T./D.M.V. enforcement man
DIFF	Different
DIIK	Damned If I Know
DIIK	Darned if I know
DIKU	Do I know You
DIKU?	Do I Know You?
DIKY	Do I Know You
DIL	Daughter-In-Law

DILLIGAD	Do I Look Like I Give A Damn?
DILLIGAF	Do I look like I give a *freak*?
DILLIGAF	Do I Look Like I Give A F**k
DILLIGAS	Do I look like I give a sugar?
DINT	Didn't
DIS	Did I say?
DIS	This
DISPATCHER BRAINS	Hauling A Very Light OR Empty Trailer
DITG	Down In The Gutter
DITYID	Did I tell you I'm distressed?
DIY	Do It Yourself
DIYD	Do It Your Dang Self
DIZ	This
DK	Don't Know
DKDC	Don't Know - Don't Care
DKM	Don't Kill Me
DKP	Dragon kill points (online gaming)
DL	Dead Last
DL	Down Load
DL	Down Low
DL	Download
DLBBB	Don't let (the) bed bugs bite
DLO	Down Low
DLTBBB	Don't Let The Bed Bugs Bite

DLTCU	Don't Let Them Catch You
DLTM	Don't lie to me
DM	Direct message
DM	Direct Message lets you send a private message to a person
DM	Direct message (Twitter slang)
DM	Do Me
DM	Doesn't matter
DM	Dungeon Master (online gaming)
DMI	Don't Mention It
DMNO	Dude Man - No Offense
DMWM	Don't Mess With Me
DMY	Don't mess yourself
DN	Double Nickel (55 MPH speed limit)
DN	Down
DNC	Does not compute (I do not understand)
DND	Do Not Disturb
DND	Donde/Where
DNFD	Do Not F**king Disturb
DNFTT	Do Not Feed The Trolls
DNO	Dude - No Offense
DNR	Dinner
DNT	Don't
DOA	Dead on Arrival
DOB	Date Of Birth
DOC	Document

DOE	Daughter of Eve
DOEI	Don't Over Engineer It
DOM	Dirty Old Man
DONT	Don't
DOOFUS	An incompetent/foolish/stupid person
DORBS	Adorable
DORK	A penis (U.S. Slang)
DORK	A socially inept person
DOUBLE NICKEL	55 Miles Per Hour
DOW	Day of Week
DOY	Day of Year
DP	Display Picture (Yahoo Messenger Chat)
DPS	Damage per second (online gaming)
DQMOT	Don't quote me on this
DQOTD	Dumb Question Of The Day
DQYDJ	Don't Quit Your Day Job
DR	Didn't read
DR	Dirty Redneck
DR	Dumb Redneck
DRAGON FLY	A Truck Who Drags Up a Hill And Flies Down
DRC	Don't Really Care
DRIVE THRU TWEET	A tweet sent from a restaurant drive-thru
DRIVE-BY-TWEET	Send between tasks
DRK	Don't Really Know
DRLNG	Darling

DRUNKTWITTERING	The act of posting on Twitter while intoxicated
DRY BOX	A Plain Freight Trailer With NO Refrigerator
DS	Darling Spouse (usually used with at least a hint of sarcasm)
DS	Dear (or Darling) son
DSI	Don't Sweat It
DSL	Desole/I'm Sorry
DSMUS	That's some messed up stuff
DT	Dang Typos
DTB	Don't text back
DTG	Dance together
DTLS	Details
DTR	Define the relationship
DTRT	Do The Right Thing
DTS	Don't think so
DTTD	Don't touch that dial
DU	Darn You
DU	Don't Understand
DUCT	Did you see that
DUK	Didn't You Know
DUNNO	Don't know
DUPE	Duplicate
DUR	Do you remember?
DUTCH	Split the cost as in Going Dutch
DUZ	Does
DUZNT	Doesn't
DV8	Deviate

DW	Darling Wife (usually used with at least a hint of sarcasm)
DW	Don't Worry
DWDIK	But What Do I Know
DWEET	Describe a tweet that has been sent by a drunk user
DWF	Divorced white female
DWIMC	Do What I Mean - Correctly!
DWIMNWIS	Do What I Mean Not What I Say
DWM	Divorced white male
DXNRY	Dictionary
DYD	Don't You Dare
DYFI	Did You Find It
DYFM	Dude you fascinate me
DYJHIW	Don't you just hate it when...?
DYK	Do You Know
DYKT	Didn't You Know That
DYNWUTB	Do you know what you are talking about?
DYOR	Do your own research (common stock market chat slang)
DYTTH	Did You Talk To Her/him
DYUT	Did You Understand That

E Codes	
E	Ecstasy
E	Enemy (online gaming)
E1	Everyone
E123	Easy as one - two - three
E2EG	Ear to ear grin
EA	Each
EAK	Eating at keyboard
EAVESTWEETING	The act of eavesdropping on other Twitter conversations
EBBSM	Engage Brain Before Starting Mouth
EBKAC	Error between keyboard and chair
ED	Erase display
EF4T	Effort
EG	Evil grin
EGOTWISTICAL	A user who talks about himself on Twitter
EI	Eat it
EIP	Editing in progress
EM	E-mail
EMA	E-mail address
EMBAR	Embarrassed/Embarrassing
EMCONS	Emoticons
EMFBI	Excuse me for butting in
EMFJI	Excuse me for jumping in
EMO	Emotion
EMSG	E-mail message
ENTK	En tout cas/In any case

ENUF	Enough
ENUFF	Enough
EOB	End of Business
EOBD	End of Business Day
EOD	End Of Day
EOD	End of discussion
EOF	End of file
EOL	End of lecture
EOL	End of Life
EOM	End of message
EOS	End of show
EOT	End of thread
EOT	End of transmission
EOTW	End of the world
EPIF	Epic Failure
EQ	Ever Quest (online gaming)
EQV	Equivalent
ER1	Everyone
ERP	Erotic Role-Play (online gaming)
ERS2	Eres tz/Are You (Spanish)
ES	Enough said
ES	Erase screen
ESAD	Eat *S* and die!
ETA	Edited to add
ETA	Estimated time (of) arrival
ETLA	Extended Three Letter Acronym
EVA	Ever

EVERY1	Everyone
Evil Kenevil	Motorcycle Cop
EVO	Evolution
EVR1	Everyone
EVRY	Every
EVRY1	Everyone
EWG	Evil wicked grin (teasing - in fun)
EWI	Emailing while intoxicated
EYC	Excitable yet calm
EZ	Easy
EZEST	Easiest
EZR	Easier
EZY	Easy

F Codes

F	Female
F2F	Face-to-Face
F2P	Free to play (online gaming)
F9	Fine
FAAK	Falling asleep at keyboard
FAB	Fabulous
FACK	Fully Acknowledged
FAF	Funny as *freak*
FAFFE	Friends are friends for ever
FAIL WHALE	A Twitter System failure image

FANKS	Thanks
FAQ	Frequently Asked Questions
FAV	Twitter feature lets you mark a person's message as a favorite
FAY	*Freak* all you
FB	Facebook
FBC	Facebook chat
FBF	Fat boy food (pizza/burgers/fries)
FBFR	Facebook friend
FBM	Fine by me
FBOW	For better or worse
FBS	F**king Bulls**t
FC	Fat Chance
FC	Fingers crossed
FC	Full card (online gaming)
FCFS	First Come First Served
FC'INGO	For crying out loud
FCOL	For crying out loud
FCU	Freaking cracking up
FEITCTAJ	*Freak* 'em if they can't take a joke
FEM	Feminine
FF	Follow Friday (Twitter slang)
FFA	Free for all (online gaming)
FFS	For *freak'*sakes
FFT	Fan-F**king-Tastic
FGI	F**king Google It

FH	Future husband
FICAR	Forget It - Cut And Run
FICCL	Frankly I couldn't care a less
FIF	*Freak* I'm funny
FIFO	First In First Out
FIIK	*Freaked* if I know
FIIOOH	Forget it - I'm out of here
FIL	Father-in-law
FIMH	Forever in my heart
FISH	First In - Still Here
FITB	Fill In The Blank
FK	French kiss
FKA	Formerly known as
FLIP FLOP	U-turn OR Return Trip
FLIPPIN	Onr of the many substitutes for F**KING
FLML	F**king Love My Life
FLS	F**king Love Sucks
FM	F**king Magic
FMF	F**k My F**king Life
FML	*Freak* My Life
FMM	F**k My Mother F**king Life
FMPOV	From My Point Of View
FMV	Fair Market Value
FN	F**k No
FNG	F**king New Guy
FO	F**k Off
FOAD	*Freak* off and die
FOAF	Friend of A Friend
FOAG	F**k Off And Google

FOBLO	Fear Of Being Left Out
FOCL	Fell off chair laughing
FOEO	For our eyes only
FOF	Fear of Failure
FOLLOWER	One who subscribes to receives your updates on Twitter
FOLLOWING	Twitter lets you see messages from all the people you follow
FOMC	Falling off my chair
FOMCL	Falling off my chair laughing
FOMO	Fear Of Missing Out
FONE	Phone
FOUR WHEELER	Car
FREAKIN	A substitute for F**KING
FREIGHT SHAKER	Freightliner Truck
FRIENDAPALOOZA	A Twitterer who adds many friends within a short time period
FRIENDSCAPPING	When an individual adds all of a friend's friends to their list
FRT	For real though
FS	F**king Sweet
FS	For Sale
FSR	For some reason
FSS	F**king Super Sweet
FSTA	Fiesta/Party
FTA	From The Article
FTASB	Faster Than A Speeding Bullet

FTBOMH	From the bottom of my heart
FTF	Face To Face
FTFA	From The F**king Article
FTFL	For The F**king Loss
FTFW	For The F**king Win
FTL	Faster Than Light
FTL	For The Loss
FTMFL	For The Mother F**king Loss
FTMFW	For The Mother F**king Win
FTS	Fan-Tan-Stic
FTW	For The Win
FTW	F**k the world
FU	*Freak* you
FU	F**k You
FU	Follow up
FUBAR	Fouled Up Beyond All Recognition
FUBAR	Fouled Up Beyond All Repair
FUBB	Fouled Up Beyond Belief
FUD	Face up deal (online gaming)
FUD	Fear/Uncertainty/Doubt
FUFL	Feel unique for life
FUG	F**king Ugly
FULL GROWN BEAR	Highway Patrol
FURTB	Full Up Ready To Burst
FW	Forward

FWB	Friend with benefits
FWIW	For What It's Worth
FWM	Fine with me
FWY	F**king With You
FX	Effects
FY	F**k Yes
FYA	For Your Amusement
FYE	For Your Entertainment
FYEO	For your eyes only
FYFI	For Your F**king Information
FYI	For Your Information

G Codes

G	Gee
G	Giggle
G	Grin
G/F	Girlfriend
G1	Good One
G2CU	Good to see you
G2G	Got to Go
G2GICYAL8ER	Got to go I'll see you later
G2R	Got to run
G2TU	Got to tell u (you)
G4C	Going for coffee
G9	Genius
GA	Go ahead
GAC	Get a clue
GAFC	Get a *freaking* clue
GAFL	Get A F**king Life

GAFMO	Get A F**king Move On
GAL	Get A Life
GAMO	Get A Move On
GAS	Got a second?
GAS	Greetings and salutations
GATEWAY CITY	St Louis MO
GAY BAY	San Francisco CA
GB	God bless
GB	Goodbye
GBA	God Bless America
GBF	Gay best friend
GBTW	Get back to work
GBU	God bless you
GD	Good
GD&R	Grinning - Ducking and Running
GD&RF	Grinning - Ducking and Running Fast
GD&WVF	Grinning - Ducking and Walking Very Fast
GD/R	Grinning - ducking/running
GDNI8	Good Night
GDR	Grinning - ducking and running
GDW	Grin - Duck and Weave
GEEK	A usually intelligent person who is socially awkward and does not fit in
GEORGIA OVERDRIVE	Shifting to Neutral going downhill to Increase

	speed
GF	Girl Friend
GFAK	Go fly a kite
GFD	God F**king Damnit
GFDI	God F**king Damn It
GFG	Good F**king Game
GFGI	Go F**king Google It
GFI	Go for it
GFL	Good F**king Luck
GFN	Gone for now
GFR	Grim File Reaper
GFS	Good F**king Story
GG	Brother (Mandarin Chinese)
GG	Good Game (online gaming)
GG	Gotta Go
GGA	Good game all (online gaming)
GGE1	Good game everyone (online gaming)
GGI	Go Google It
GGMSOT	Gotta get me some of that
GGN	Gotta go now
GGOH	Gotta Get Outa Here
GGP	Gotta Go Pee
GGU2	Good game - you too
GH	Good hand (online gaming)
GI	Google It
GIAR	Give it a rest

GIAYG	Give it all you got
GIC	Gift in crib (online gaming)
GIDK	Gee I Don't Know
GIGO	Garbage In - Garbage Out
GIL	Get In Line
GIMME	Give me
GIRL	Guy in real life
GIWIST	Gee I Wish I'd Said That
GJ	Good job
GJP	Good job partner
GL	Good Luck
GL/HF	Good luck - have fun (online gaming)
GL2U	Good luck to you (online gaming)
GLA	Good luck all (online gaming)
GLE	Good luck everyone (online gaming)
GLE1	Good luck everyone (online gaming)
GLGH	Good Luck and Good Hunting
GLNG	Good luck next game (online gaming)
GLWTN	Guffawing loudly waking up the neighborhood
GM	Good Morning
GMAB	Give Me A Break
GMAO	Giggling my A$$ off
GMBO	Giggling my butt off

GMFAB	Give Me A F**king Break
GMTA	Great Minds Think Alike
GMV	Got my vote
GN	Good night
GN8	Good night
GNA	Good night all
GNE1	Good night everyone
GNIGHT	Good night
G'NIGHT	good night
GNITE	Good night
GNO	Girls' Night Out
GNSD	Good night - Sweet dreams
GNSTDLTBBB	Good night sleep tight don't let the bed bugs bite
GNU	Good - N' You?
GO	Get Out or Get Off
GO2	Go to
GOI	Get over it
GOIA	Get over it already
GOIN	Going
GOL	Giggling out loud
GOMB	Get off my back
GONNA	Going to
GOOD BUDDY	Now Used As A Term For A Homosexual
GOOH	Get out of here
GOSTA	Got to
GOTCHA	Got you
GOWI	Get On With It
GOYFA	Get Off Your Fat Ass

GPOY	Gratuitous picture of yourself
GR&D	Grinning Running and Ducking
GR8	Great
GR8FL	Great for life
GRANNY LANE	Slow Lane
GRATZ	Congratulations
GREASY SIDE UP	A Car With It's Wheels In The Air
GREASY STUFF	Snow or Ice
GRGZ	Gorgeous
GRL	Girl
GROUND PRESSURE	Weight Of A Truck
GRRR	Enfadado/Angry
GRWG	Get right with God
GS	Good shot
GS	Good split (online gaming)
GS	Good Story
GSTK	God Save The King
GSTQ	God Save The Queen
GT	Good try
GTAH	Go take a hike
GTAW	Go take a walk
GTCU	Glad to see you
GTFG	Go To F**king Google
GTFH	Go To F**king Hell
GTFO	Get the *freak* out
GTFOH	Get the *freak* outta here

GTFOML	Get the frick outtta my life
GTG	Go To Google
GTG	Good to go
GTG	Got To Go
GTGEMB	Got to go eat my breakfast
GTGEMD	Got to go eat my dinner
GTGEML	Got to go eat my lunch
GTGTS	Got to go to sleep
GTH	Go to heck
GTH	Go To Hell
GTL	Get a life
GTLD	Get a life dude
GTM	Giggling to myself
GTRM	Going to read mail
GTSY	Great (or good) to see you
GUD	Good
GUITAR CITY	Nashville TN
GWHTLC	Glad we had this little chat

H Codes

H	Hug
H&K	Hugs & kisses
H/O	Hold on
H2CUS	Hope to see you soon
H2E	Have to eat
H2H	Hard to hear
H2SO4	Sulfuric Acid - refers to

	someone with a caustic attitude
H4U	Hot For You
H8	Hate
H8TTU	Hate to be you
HAAK	How about a kiss
HAAT	Sexy or attractive
HADG	Have a great day
HAFTA	Have to
HAG1	Have a good one
HAGD	Have A Great Day
HAGN	Have a good night
HAGO	Have a good one
HAGS	Have a great summer
HAK	Hugs And Kisses
HALOOO	Hello
HAMMER DOWN	Move Faster
HAMMER LANE	Left Lane [Fast Lane]
HAND	Driver
HAND	Have A Nice Day
HANDLE	Nickname (Userid or CB nickname)
HASH TAG	A hash tag (hashtag) is a way of organizing your updates
HAU	How about you?
HAV2	Have to
HAWT	Have a wonderful day
HAX	Hacks
HB	Hug back
HBASTD	Hitting Bottom And Starting To Dig

H-BDAY	Happy Birthday
HBH	Hoes be Hoes
HBS	Hurry back soon
HBU	How 'bout you?
HC	Holy Cow
HDYLTA	How Do You Like Them Apples?
HED	Head
HED	Hello everyone
HF	Have fun
HFAC	Holy flipping animal crackers
H-FDAY	Happy Father's Day
HFS	Holy F**king S**t
HHHVF	Ha ha ha very funny
HHIS	Hanging Head In Shame
HHOJ	Ha Ha Only Joking
HHOK	Ha Ha Only Kidding
HHTYAY	Happy Holidays to You and Yours
HIM	Hotmail Instant Messenger
HIVEMIND	Refers to the combined intelligence of all Twitter users
HL	Half Life (online gaming)
HLA	Hola/Hello (Spanish)
HM	Home Work
H-MDAY	Happy Mother's Day
HMU	Contact me to follow up - Hit Me Up
HMWRK	Homework

HND	Have a nice day
HNL	(w)Hole 'nother level
HNY	Happy New Year
HNY	Happy New Year
HOAS	Hang On A Second
HOE	A skank; a slut; a person (male or female) who would f**k anything
HOLA	Hello (Spanish)
HOME 20	Your Home
HOS	Husband over shoulder
HOYEW	Hanging On Your Every Word
HP	Helicopter Parents
HP	Hit points / Health points (online gaming)
HRU	How are you?
HS	Holy S**t
HSIK	How Should I Know
HSX	Hey sexy
HT	Hi There
HTH	Hope That Helps!
HTRD	Hard to recognize dude
HU	Hurry up
HUBH	Head up butt head
HUD	How you doing?
HUS	Husband
HUYA	Head up your *butt*
HV	Have
HVH	Heroic Violent Hold (online gaming)
HW	Homework

HYFR	How You Feel Really?
i<3u	I love you
I2	I too (me too)
IA8	I already ate
IAAA	I am an accountant
IAAD	I am a doctor
IAAL	I am a lawyer
IAC	In Any Case
IAE	In Any Event
IAMOS	In a Manner of Speaking
IANAC	I am not a crook
IANAL	I Am Not A Lawyer (but)
IANALB	I Am Not A Lawyer but ….
IAO	I am out (of here)
IAW	In Accordance With
IB	I'm back
IBD	In Before Dark
IBK	Idiot Behind Keyboard
IBTD	I Beg To Differ
IBTL	In Before the Lock
IBU	I believe you
IBYP	I beg your pardon
I Codes	
IC	I See
ICAM	I couldn't agree more
ICBW	It could be worse
ICEDI	I can't even discuss it
ICFILWU	I could fall in love with

	you
ICW	I can't wait
ICYMI	In case you missed it (Twitter slang)
IDBI	I don't believe it
IDC	I Don't Care
IDFC	I Don't F**king Care
IDFGAS	I Don't F**king Give A S**t
IDFK	I Don't F**king Know
IDGAD	I don't give a darn
IDGAF	I don't give a *freak*
IDGAS	I Don't Give A S**t
IDGI	I don't get it
IDK	I Don't Know
IDKTMWIM	I Don't Know Tell Me What It Means
IDNO	I don't know
IDR	I Don't Remember
IDRC	I don't really care
IDRK	I don't really know
IDT	I don't think
IDTS	I don't think so
IDUNNO	I don't know
IDW2TAI	I don't want to talk about it
IDWTTU	I don't wanna talk to you
IDY	I dare you
IFC	In F**king Control
IFHML	I F**king Hate My Life
IFHU	I F**king Hate You
IFLU	I F**king Love You

83

IFLY	I F**king Love You
IFLY	I forever love you
IFYP	I feel your pain
IG2R	I got to run
IGAF	I Give a F**K
IGHT	I got high tonight
IGN	I (I've) got nothing
IGP	I got to (go) pee
IGT	I Got This
IGTG	I got to go
IH2G	I have to go
IHML	I Hate My Life
IHNC	I Have No Clue
IHNFC	I Have No F**king Clue
IHNI	I have no idea
IHTFP	I Hate This F**king Place
IHTP	I Hate This Place
IHU	I Hate You
IHU	I hear u
IHUSFM	I Hate You So F**king Much
IHUSM	I Hate You So Much
IIABDFI	If It Ain't Broke DON'T Fix It
IIIO	Intel inside/idiot outside
IIRC	If I Recall Correctly...
IIRC	If I Remember Correctly
IIWM	If It Were Me
IIWY	If I Were You
IJ	In Jail
IJF	I just farted
IJWTK	I Just Want To Know

IJWTS	I Just Want To Say
IK	I know
IKI	I knew it
IKR	I know right?
IKT	I know that
IKU	I know you
IKWR	I Know What's Right
IKWUM	I Know What You Mean
IKWW	I Know What's Wrong
IKYABWAI	I Know You Are But What Am I?
ILBL8	I'll be late
ILL	I'll
ILMFL	I Love My F**king Life
ILML	I Love My Life
ILQ	I like you
ILU	I Love You
ILUM	I love you man
ILUM	I love you more
ILUSFM	I Love You So F**king Much
ILUSFM	I love you so freaking much
ILUSM	I Love You So Much
ILY	I Love You
ILY2	I love you too
ILYH	I love you harder
ILYSM	I love you so much
IM	Instant Messager
IMA	I Might Add
IMAHO	In My Absolutely Honest Opinion

IMAO	In My Arrogant Opinion
IMBO	In My Biased Opinion
IMCO	In My Considered Opinion
IME	In My Experience
IMFO	In My F**king Opinion
IMHO	In My Humble Opinion
IMN2U	I'm Into You
IMNSHO	In My Not So Humble Opinion
IMO	In My Opinion
IMPOV	In My Point Of View
IMS	I am sorry
IMSB	I am so bored
IMTM	I am the man
IMU	I miss u (you)
IMYSFM	I Miss You So F**king Much
IMYSM	I Miss You So Much
IN2HYF	I need to hold you forever
INAL	I'm not a lawyer
INC	Incoming (online gaming)
INDY 500	Indianapolis IN
INET	Internet
INO	I know
INPO	In No Particular Order
INTWITUATED	Someone who is infatuated with another Twitter user
INTWITUATION	The condition of being infatuated with another

	Twitter user
INV	Invite
IOH	I'm Outta Here
IOHE4U	I Only Have Eyes For You
IOMH	In over my head
IOU	I owe you
IOW	In Other Words
IRDC	I really don't care
IRDK	I really don't know
IRL	In Real Life
IRMC	I rest my case
IRT	In Regards To
ISLY	I still love you
ISP	Internet Service Provider
ISS	I'm So Sure
ISSYGTI	I'm So Sure You Get The Idea!
ISWYM	I See What You Mean
ITAM	It's The Accounting Man (financial blogs)
ITFA	In The Final Analysis
ITIKT	I think I know that
ITN	I Think Not
ITRW	In The Real World
ITSFWI	If The Shoe Fits Wear It
ITT	In this thread
ITYK	I thought you knew
ITYKT	I Thought You Knew That
IUKWIM	If you know what I mean
IUSS	If you say so

IWALU	I Will Always Love You
IWAWO	I want a way out
IWBNI	It Would Be Nice If
IWIAM	Idiot wrapped in a moron
IWKYL	I will key you later
IWTAAQ	I Want To Ask A Question
IWUWH	I wish you were here
IYFEG	Insert Your Favorite Ethnic Group
IYKWIM	If you know what I mean
IYO	In your opinion
IYSS	If You Say So
IYSWIM	If You See What I Mean

J Codes

J/A	Just asking
J/K	Joking
J/P	Just playing
J/W	Just wondering
J00	You
J00R	Your
J2LUK	Just to let you know
J4F	Just For Fun
J4G	Just for giggles
JA2ND	Just a second
JAA	Just Another Animal
JAFA	Just Another F**king Animal
JAFO	Just Another F**king Observer

JAM	Just A Minute
JAO	Just Another Observer
JAS	Just A Second
JC	Just checking
JC	Just Chilling
JDI	Just Do It
JE LE SAV	Je le savais/I knew it
JELLY	Jealous
JFDI	Just F**king Do It
JFF	Just For Fun
JFGI	Just F**king Google It
JFI	Just For Information
JFWY	Just F**king With You
JFYI	Just for your information
JGI	Just Google It
JIC	Just In Case
JJ	Just joking
JJA	Just joking around
JK	Just Kidding
JLMK	Just let me know
JLT	Just like that
JLU	Jesus loves you
JM	Just messing
JMHO	Just My Humble Opinion
JMO	Just My Opinion
JP	Jackpot (online gaming)
JP	Just playing
JSI	Just say it
JST	Just stop talking
JT	Just teasing
JTLUK	Just to let you know
JTLYK	Just to let you know

JV	Joint venture
JW	Just wondering
JWJ	Jumping with joy
JWK	Just Wondering

K Codes

K	OK
K/B	Keyboard
KB	Keyboard
KB	Kick butt (online gaming)
KEEP SHINY SIDE UP/THE RUBBER SIDE DOWN	Have a safe trip
KEWL	Cool
KEYME	Key me (when you get in)
KFY	Kiss for you
KHYF	Know How You Feel
KIA	Killed In Action
KIA	Know it all
KIBO	Knowledge In - Bullshit Out
KISS	Keep It Simple Stupid
KISS	Keep it Sweetly Simple
KIT	Keep In Touch
KJST	OK - Just Stop Talking
KK	Okay! Okay!
KL	Cool
KLS	Class
KLU	Cool like you
KM	Kiss me

KMA	Kiss my *a*
KMFA	Kiss My F**king A$$
KMIA	Kiss My Italian Ass
KMK	Kiss my keister
KMT	Kiss my tushie
KN	Knocked Up (pregnant)
KNIM	Know what I mean?
KNOW	Knowledge
KOC	Kiss on cheek
KOL	Kiss on lips
KOS	Kid over shoulder
KOS	Pussy (Persian/Farsi similar to F**k)
KOTC	Kiss on the cheek
KOTL	Kiss On The Lips
KOW	Knock on wood
KP	Cut and Paste
KPC	Keep Parents Clueless
KS	Kill then steal (online gaming)
K-Town	Knoxville TN
KUTGW	Keep up the good work
KWIM	Know What I Mean?
KWL	Cool
KYFC	Keep Your Fingers Crossed

L Codes

L	Laugh
L2G	Like to go?
L2G	Love to go

L2K	Like to come
L2P	Learn to play
L2S	Laughing to self
L8	Late
L8R	Later
L8RG8R	Later gator
LABATYD	Life's A Bitch - Then You Die
LAL	Laugh a little
LANDLINE	Wired Telephone
LARGE CAR	Very Fast Nice Truck
LBAY	Laughing back at you
LBNOL	Laughing but not out loud
LBR	Loser beyond repair
LBS	Laughing but serious
LBVS	Laughing but very serious
LD	Later dude
LD	Long Day
LD	Long distance
LDO	Like duh! Obviously!
LEFT COAST	West Coast
LEMENO	Let me know
LERK	Leaving easy reach of keyboard
LERKR	Eavesdropping on social media without participating
LFD	Left for day
LFD	Long F**king Day
LFG	Looking for group (online

	gaming)
LFM	Looking for more (online gaming)
LGH	Let's get high
LH6	Let's have sex
LHM	Lord help me
LHO	Laughing head off
LHSX	Let's have sex
LHU	Lord help us
LI	LinkedIn
LIC	Like I care
LIFO	Last In First Out
LIG	Life is good
LIK	Liquor
LIL	Little
LIMT	Laugh in my tummy
LIS	Life is short
LIU	Livin it up
LJBF	Let's Just Be Friends
LLAP	Live Long And Prosper
LLGB	Love - Later God bless
LLTA	Lots and Lots of Thunderous Applause
LM	Love me
LMA	Leave Me Alone
LMAO	Laughing My A$$ Off
LMBO	Laugh My Butt Off
LMFAO	Laughing My F**king A$$ Off
LMFAO	Laughing my fat a** off
LMFAO	Laughing my freaking *a* off

LMHO	Laughing My Head Off
LMIRL	Let's meet in real life
LMK	Let Me Know
LML	Love My Life
LMNK	Leave my name out
LMS	Let Me See
LMS	Like my status (Facebook)
LMSO	Laughing my socks off
LNS	Laughing non stop
LNT	Lost in translation
LOA	List of acronyms
LOFL	Laughing Out F**king Loud
LOL	Laughing Out Loud
LOL	Lots of Love
LOL	Lots Of Luck
LOLH	Laughing out loud hysterically
LOLOV	Lots of love
LOLV	Lot's Of Love
LOML	Love Of My Life
LOT LIZARD	Truck stop hooker
LOTI	Laughing on the inside
LOTR	Lord of The Rings (online gaming)
LQL	Laughing Quite Loudly
LQTM	Laughing Quietly To Myself
LRO	Let's rock on
LS	Love Sucks
LSFH	Laughing So F**king

	Hard
LSH	Laughing So Hard
LSHMBH	Laughing So Hard My Belly Hurts
LSMFT	Loose Straps Mean Floppy T*ts
LSV	Language - Sex and violence
LT8R	Later
LTD	Living the dream
LTHTT	Laughing Too Hard To Type
LTM	Laughing To Myself
LTNS	Long Time No See
LTNT	Long Time No Type
LTOD	Laptop of death
LTR	Later
LTS	Laughing to Self
LTY	Laughing to Yourself
LULT	Love you long time
LUWAMH	Love You With All My Heart
LVM	Left voice mail
LWOS	Laughing without smiling
LY	Love ya
LY	Love You
LYK	Like
LYL	Love you lots
LYLAB	Love You Like A Brother
LYLAS	Love You Like A Sister
LYLC	Love you like crazy
LYMY	Love You Miss You

LYSFM	Love You So F**king Much
LYSM	Love You So Much

M Codes

M	Male
M$	Microsoft
M/B	My bad
M2F	More to follow
M8	Mate
MAD	Make a decision
MB	Mamma's boy
MBIL	My Boss Is Listening
MBN	Must be nice
MBS	Mom behind shoulder
MC	Merry Christmas
MDC	My dad's calling
MDIAC	My Dad is a cop
MEAT-WAGON	Ambulance
MEGO	My Eyes Glaze Over
MEH	Shrugging shoulders
MEHH	Sigh or sighing
MENTION	Used to name another user within your tweet
MEZ	Mesmerizing (online gaming)
MFB	Mother F**king Bitch
MFC	My friend calls
MFI	Mad for it
MFMF	Mother F**king Mother F**ker

MGB	May God bless
MGIS	Money growth info systems
MGMT	Management
MHB2U	My heart belongs to you
MHO	My Honest Opinion
MIA	Missing In Action
MICROBLOG	A type of blog that lets users publish short text updates
MICROBLOGGING	Using services such as Twitter to update your blog
MICROFUNDING	Using social media microblogging to raise money
MICROPOST	Posts published by micro bloggers
MIM	Mission Impossible
MIM	Mission Improbable
MIN	Minute
MIRL	Meet in real life
MISTWEET	A tweet that you later regret having sent
MJ	Mary Jane (Marijuana)
MKAY	Mmm - Okay
ML8TR	More later
MLA	Multiple Letter Acronym
MM	Sister (Mandarin Chinese)
MMB	Message Me Back
MMC	My mom's calling
MMO	Massively Multiplayer

	Online
MMORPG	Massively Multiplayer Online Role-Playing Games
MMW	Mark my words
MNSG	Mensaje/Message (Spanish)
MOB	Mobile
MOD	Moderator
MOF	Male or Female
MOF	Matter Of Fact
MOMBOY	Mamma's boy
MOO	Matter Of Opinion
MOO	My own opinion
MOOS	Member Of The Opposite Sex
MORF	Male or female?
MOS	Mom Over Shoulder
MOSS	Member Of Same Sex
MOTAS	Member Of The Appropriate Sex
MOTD	Message of the day
MOTION LOTION	Diesel Fuel
MOTOR CITY	Detroit MI
MOTOS	Member Of The Opposite Sex
MOTSS	Member Of The Same Sex
MP	Mana points (online gaming)
MRA	Moving Right Along
MRT	Modified Retweet

MS	Manuscript
MSG	Message
MSTK	Sender made a mistake typing their last message
MT	Mistell (mistaken chat message - please disregard)
MTF	More to follow
MTFBWU	May the force be with you
MTG	Meeting
MTTSKG	Multitasking
MTTSKR	Multi-tasker
MU	Miss U (you)
MUAAH	Multiple unsuccessful attempts (at/to) humor
MUAL	Missing you a lot
MUSM	Miss you so much
MV	Music video
MWAH	Kiss (mimics the sound made when kissing through the air)
MWLB	Made with love by
MYO	Mind your own (business)
MYOB	Mind Your Own Business
MYODB	Mind your own darn business
MYOFB	Mind Your Own F**king Business
MYS	Miss you so

N Codes	
N	And
N	In
N/C	No Comment
N/M	Not much
N/W	No way
N/Y	Not yet
N00B	Newbie
N1	Nice one
N2M	Not too much
N2M	Nothing too much
N2N	Nice to know
N8	Night
NA	Not Applicable
NA	Not Available
NAC	Not A Clue
NADT	Not a darn thing
NAFC	Not A F**king Clue
NAFTA	North American Free Trade Agreement
NALOPKT	Not a lot of people know that
NAVY	Never Again Volunteer Yourself
NBD	No Big Deal
NBFAB	Not bad for a beginner (online gaming)
NBSB	No boyfriend since birth
NC	Nice crib (online gaming)
NC	No Clue
NC	No Comment
NCE1	Nice one

ND	Nice double (online gaming)
ND	No Doubt
NDBWY	Nice doing business with you
NE	Any
NE1	Anyone
NE14KFC?	Anyone for KFC?
NEC	Not even close
NEHOW	Anyhow
NEMORE	Anymore
NERD	An intelligent but single-minded person obsessed with a nonsocial hobby o r pursuit
NERF	Changed and is now weaker (online gaming)
NEWBIE	New person with limited skills
NEWEETER	A new Twittter user
NFC	No F**king Clue
NFD	No F**king Doubt
NFG	No F**king Good
NFM	None for me
NFM	Not for me
NFP	No F**king Problem
NFS	Need for Speed (online gaming)
NFS	Not for sale
NFW	No *freaking* way
NFW	Not for work
NG	New Guy

NG	No Good
NGH	Not gonna happen
NGL	Not gonna lie
NGNG	No guts - No glory
NGSB	No girlfriend since birth
NH	Nice hand (online gaming)
NHOH	Never Heard Of Him/Her
NHOT	Never heard of that
NI	No idea
NIFOC	Naked in front of computer
NIGI	Now I get it
NIH	Not Invented Here
NIMBY	Not in My Back Yard
NIMU	No I meant u
NIMY	No I meant you
NINO	Nothing In - Nothing Out
NIROK	Not in reach of keyboard
NITFM	Not In The F**king Mood
NITM	Not In The Mood
NK	No kidding
NL	Nose laugh
NLT	No later than
NM	Never Mind
NM	Nice meld (online gaming)
NM	Not Much
NM	Nothing much
NMFP	Not My F**king Problem
NMH	Not much here
NMJC	Nothing much just

	chilling
NMN	Not my number
NMO	Not My Opinion
NMP	Not My Problem
NMU	Not much - You?
NNTR	No need to reply
NO1	No one
NOMW	Not On My Watch
NON	Now or never
NOOB	A beginner - Someone who is bad at (online) games
NORTH BOUND HEADING SOUTH	Wrong way driver
NOWL	Knowledge
NOYB	None Of Your Business
NOYFB	None Of Your F**king Business
NP	No Problem
NPA	No permanent address
NPC	Non-playing character (online gaming)
NPN	No Pasa Nada/Nothing's happening (Spanish)
NQA	No Questions Asked
NQT	Newly qualified teacher
NR	Nice roll (online gaming)
NRN	No reply necessary
NRN	No Response Necessary
NS	Nice score (online gaming)
NS	Nice split (online gaming)

NSA	No strings attached
NSFW	Not safe for work
NSFW	Not safe for work
NSFW	Not Safe For Workplace Viewing
NSISR	Not sure if spelled right
NSTAAFL	No Such Thing As A Free Lunch
NT	Nice try
NTCU	Nice to see you
NTE	Not that easy
NTIM	Not That It Matters
NTIMM	Not That It Matters Much
NTMU	Nice to meet you
NTN	No Thanks Needed
NTPBL	Not possible
NTS	Note to self
NTU	No Thank You
NTW	Not To Worry
NTY	No Thank You
NTYMI	Now That You Mention It
NV	Envy
NVM	Never Mind
NVNG	Nothing ventured - Nothing gained
NVR	Never
NVRFM	Never F**king Mind
NVRM	Never Mind
NW	Network
NW	No way
NWO	No way out
NWOT	New With Out Tags

NWT	New With Tags
NY	Not yet
NYB	Not Your Business
NYT	Night

O Codes

O	Hugs (as in hugs and kisses XOXO)
O	Opponent (online gaming)
O	Over (indicates the end of a communication)
O:-)	Angelic
O4U	Only for you
OA	Online auctions
OATUS	On a Totally Unrelated Subject
OAUS	On An Unrelated Subject
OB	Obligatory
OB	Oh baby
OB	Oh boy
OB	Oh brother
OBO	Or Best Offer
OBTW	Oh By The Way
OBV	Obviously
OFC	Of course
OFW	Oh F**king Well
OG	Original gangster
OGIM	Oh God it's Monday
OH	Over Heard
OI	Operator indisposed

OIB	Oh - I'm back
OIC	Oh I See
OINYW	Oh I know you will
OJ	Only joking
OJ	Orange Juice
OKC	Oh - Ok cool
OL	Old lady
OL	Online
OLL	Online love
OM	Oh my
OM	Old man
OMAA	Oh my aching *A*
OMAB	Oh my aching butt
OMDB	Over my dead body
OMFG	Oh my *freaking* God
OMFW	Oh My F**king Word
OMG	Oh Mother God
OMG	Oh My God
OMG	Oh my gosh
OMGYG2BK	Oh my God you got to be kidding
OMGYS	Oh my gosh you suck
OMS	(Promise) On my soul
OMW	Oh My Word
OMW	On my way
ONL	Online
ONNA	Oh No Not Again
ONNTA	Oh No Not This Again
ONYD	Oh No You Didn't
OO	Over and Out (used in Chats and IM to signal end of communication)

OOAK	One of a Kind
OOB	Out of body
OOC	Out of character
OOH	Out of here
OOK	Oh okay
OOM	Out of mind
OOTC	Obligatory On-Topic Comment
OOTD	One of these days
OOTO	Out of the office
OP	On phone
OP	Original Poster (the one who started this discussion thread)
OP	Out of place
ORLY	Oh really?
OS	Operating system
OST	On Second Thought
OT	Off topic (discussion forums)
OT	Over Time
OTB	Off to bed
OTF	On the Floor (laughing)
OTL	Out To Lunch
OTOH	On the Other Hand
OTOOH	On The Other Other Hand
OTP	On the phone
OTT	Over The Top
OTTH	On The Third Hand
OTTOMH	Off The Top Of My Head
OTW	Off to work

OVA	Over
OW	Oh Well
OWTH	Oh What the heck
OWTTE	Or Words To That Effect
OYO	On your own

P Codes

P	Partner (online gaming)
P2P	Parent to parent
P2P	Pay to play (online gaming)
P2P	Peer to peer
P911	Parent Alert Change Subject
P911	Parents coming into room alert
PABG	Packing a Big Gun
PAC	Parents are coming
PARKING LOT	A truck hauling cars
PAT	Patrol (online gaming)
PAW	Parents are watching
PBOOK	Phonebook (e-mail)
PC	Player character (online gaming)
PCM	Please call me
PCMCIA	People Can't Memorize Computer Industry Acronyms
PCO	Poco/A little (Spanish)
PCT	Podcasting
PD	Public Domain

PDA	Personal display (of) affection
PDH	Pretty damn happy
PDH	Pretty darn happy
PDND	Please do not disturb
PDQ	Pretty Damn Quick
PDS	Please don't shoot
PDS	Please Don't Shout!(for those using All Caps)
PDT	Pierdete/Get lost (Spanish)
PEBCAK	Problem Encountered Between Chair And Keyboard (describes an inept operator)
PEEPS	People
PFG	Pretty F**king Good
PFM	Please Forgive Me
PFM	Pure F**king Magic
PFT	Pretty *freaking* tight
PG	Pretty Good
PH	Pretty Hot
PHAT	Pretty Hot And Tempting
PIA	Pain In (the) A$$
PIC	Picture
PICKLE PARK	Rest Area
PIP	Peeing in pants (laughing hard)
PIR	Parents in room
PISS	Put in some sugar
PITA	Pain in the *butt*
PITA	Pain In The A$$

PJ	Private joke
PK	Player Kill
PKMN	Pokemon (online gaming)
PL8	Plate
PLD	Played
PLMK	Please let me know
PLOKTA	Press Lots Of Keys To Abort
PLOS	Parent looking over shoulder
PLS	Please
PLU	People like us
PLZ	Please
PLZTLME	Please tell me
PM	Private Message
PM	Pure Magic
PMBI	Pardon My Barging In
PMBI	Pardon My Breaking In
PMBI	Pardon My Butting In
PMF	Pardon My French
PMF	Pure Freaking Magic
PMFBI	Pardon Me For Barging In
PMFBI	Pardon Me For Breaking In
PMFBI	Pardon Me For Butting In
PMFI	Pardon me for interrupting
PMFI	Pardon my interrupting
PMFJI	Pardon Me For Jumping In

PMIGBOM	Put Mind In Gear BEFORE Opening Mouth
PMJI	Pardon My Jumping In
PMM	Private Message me
PMP	Peeing My Pants
PMS	Pre Menstrual Syndrome
PMSL	Pee myself laughing
PNCAH	Please! No Cursing Allowed Here
PNM	Piss and Moan
POAHF	Put on a happy face
POC	Piece Of Crap
POETS	Piss on everything tomorrow is Saturday
POH	Parents over heard
POIDH	Picture or it didn't happen
POLE CAT	Skunk
POMC	Peck on my cheek
POOF	Goodbye
POOSSLQ	Person Of Opposite Sex Sharing Living Quarters
PORN	Pornography
POS	Parents Over Shoulder (Sender is under scrutiny)
POS	Piece of S**t
POT	Potion (online gaming)
POTUS	President of the United States
POV	Point of view
POV	Privately owned vehicle (not a gov't vehicle)

PPL	People
PPR	Paper
PPU	Pending pick-up
PRB	Probably
PRESH	Precious
PRL	Parents are listening
PROB	Problem
PROBLY	Probably
PROBS	Probably
PROGGY	Computer program
PROGMR	Computer programmer
PROLLY	Probably
PRT	Please Retweet
PRTY	Party
PRW	People/parents are watching
PSOS	Parent standing over shoulder
PSP	PlayStation Portable
PST	Please send tell (online gaming)
PTFO	Pass the *freak* out
PTIYPASI	Put that in your pipe and smoke it
PTL	Praise the Lord
PTMM	Please Tell Me More
PTO	Paid time off
PTO	Parent Teacher Organization
PTO	Personal time off
PTTMIAB	Please talk to me - I am bored

PU	That stinks!
PUG	Pick up group (online gaming)
PUKS	Pick up kids
PVP	Player versus player (online gaming)
PWN	Pawn
PXT	Please explain that
PYT	Pretty young thing
PZ	Peace
PZA	Pizza

Q Codes

Q	Queue
Q4U	(I have a) question for you
QAF	Tell me when you arrive
QAI	How is traffic
QAM	What's the weather forecast
QC	Quality control
QFE	Question for everyone
QFI	Quoted for idiocy
QFI	Quoted for irony
QFMFT	Quoted for Mother F**king Truth
QFT	Quoted For Truth
QIK	Quick
QL	Quit laughing
QOTD	Quote of the day
QQ	Quick question

QRA	Who are you
QRB	How far away are you
QRD	Where are you going
QRK	Do you hear me
QRL	Are you busy
QSED	Quick/Simple/Easily Done
QSL	Reply
QSO	Conversation
QT	Cutie
QT	Quit Talking
QTF	Quit F**king Talking
QTPI	Cutie pie
QUEEN CITY	Charlotte NC
QUES	Question

R Codes

R	Are
R U THERE	Are you there?
R2U	Roses to you
R8	Rate
RADIO CK	Does My Radio Work?
RAEBNC	Read And Enjoyed But No Comment
RBAY	Right back at you
RBF	Relaxed Bitch Face
RE	Hello again
RE	In Regard To
RE	Regarding
REHI	Hi again
REM	Remember

RFMH	Reason for my happiness
RFN	Right F**king Now
RGR	Roger (as in roger that/I understand)
RGS	Regards
RHIP	Rank Has Its Privileges
RIP	Rest in peace
RL	Real Life
RLCO	Real Life Conference
RLY	Really
RM	Room
RME	Rolling my eyes
RMLB	Read my lips baby
RMMM	Read my mail man
RN	Right Now
RNN	Reply not needed
RNR	Reply not required
ROFBNL	Rolling on the floor but not laughing
ROFL	Rolling On Floor Laughing
ROFLAS	Rolling On Floor Laughing And Screaming
ROFLAY	Rolling on the floor laughing at you
ROFLCOPTER	Rolling on floor laughing and spinning around
ROFLMAO	Roll On Floor Laughing My A** Off
ROFLMFAO	Rolling On The Floor Laughing My F**king A$$ Off

ROFLOL	Roll On Floor Laughing Out Loud
ROFLUTS	Rolling on the floor laughing unable to speak
ROFLWTIME	Rolling on the floor laughing with tears in my eyes
ROFMO	Rolling on the floor making out
ROI	Return on Investment
ROMFT	Roll On Mother F**king Tide
ROT	Roll On Tide
ROTF	Rolling On The Floor
ROTFFL	Rolling On F**king Floor Laughing
ROTFL	Rolling On The Floor Laughing
ROTFLMAO	Rolling On The Floor Laughing My A$$ Off
ROTFLMAOTID	Rolling On The Floor Laughing My A** Off Till I Die
ROTFLOL	Rolling On The Floor Laughing Out Loud
ROTFLTIC	Rolling On The Floor Laughing Till I Cry
ROTFLUTS	Rolling on the floor laughing unable to speak
ROX	rocks
RPG	Role Playing Game
RRQ	Return Receipt Request
RS	Runescape (online

	gaming)
RSN	Real soon now
RSVP	Respondez S'il Vous Plait-French for Please Reply
RT	Real Time
RT	Retweet (Twitter slang)
RT	Roger that
RTA	Read the Article
RTBM	Read The Bloody Manual
RTBS	Reason to be single
RTD	Read The Description
RTF	Read The FAQ
RTFA	Read the F**king Article
RTFAQ	Read The Frequently Asked Questions
RTFD	Read The F**king Description
RTFF	Read The Freaking FAQ
RTFI	Read The F**king Instructions
RTFM	Read the *freaking* manual
RTFM	Read The F------ Manual
RTFT	Read The F**king Thread
RTHX	Thanks for the RT (Retweet)
RTI	Read The Instructions
RTM	Read The Manual
RTMS	Read the manual stupid
RTNTN	Retention

RTQ	Read The Question
RTRCTV	Retroactive
RTRMT	Retirement
RTSM	Read The Silly Manual
RTSM	Read the stupid manual
RTT	Read The Thread
RTWFQ	Read the whole *freaking* question
RU	Are you?
RUFKM	Are You F**king Kidding Me
RUFR	Are You For Real
RUFRE	Are u free
RUKM	Are You Kidding Me
RUMOF	Are you male or female?
RUOK	Are You OK?
RUS	Are You Serious
RUT	Are u (you) there?
RW	Real World
RWSQ	Are We Square
RX	Drugs or prescriptions
RYB	Read your Bible
RYC	Are You Coming
RYFM	Read Your Friendly Manual
RYO	Roll your own
RYS	Are you single?
RYS	Read Your Screen
S Codes	
S	Smile

S2PID	Stupid
S2R	Send to receive (send me your picture to get mine)
S2S	Sorry to say
S4L	Spam for life
SA	Smart a**
SA	Special Agent (usually sarcasm)
SA	Stupid Acronyms
SAL	Such a laugh
SALT SHAKER	Snow Plow
SAPFU	Surpassing All Previous Foul Ups
SAT	Sorry about that
SB	Should be
SB	Smiling back
SB	So Bored
SBIA	Standing back in amazement
SBT	Sorry 'bout that
SC	Stay cool
SCNR	Sorry! Could Not Resist!
SCOTUS	Supreme Court of the United States
SD	Sweet dreams
SDMB	Sweet dreams my baby
SEAT COVER	Female passenger
SEC	Wait a second
SELFIE	A photo that is taken of oneself for social media sharing

SENPAI	Someone older you look up to
SESAME STREET	CB Channel 19
SETE	Smiling Ear To Ear
SF	So Funny
SFAIK	So far as I know
SFB	S**t For Brains
SFB	So F**king Bored
SFF	So F**king Funny
SFG	Search F**king Google
SFL	Sister for life
SFLA	Stupid Four Letter Acronym
SFLR	Sorry for the late reply
SFSG	So Far So Good
SFW	So F**king What
SG	Search Google
SGTM	Sounds Good To Me
SH	Same here
SH^	Shut up
Shake The Bushes	Run Ahead Of Others To Lure Out The Bears
SHAKY-TOWN	Los Angeles CA
SHID	Slapping head in disgust
SHOOTING YOU IN THE BACK	Police Out Of Sight Hitting You With Radar
SHORT SHORT	Short Time
SIAP	Sorry If Already Posted
SICNR	Sorry I could not resist
SICS	Sitting In Chair Snickering
SIG2R	Sorry I got to run

SIHTH	Stupidity is hard to take
SIL	Sister-In-Law
SIMCS	Sitting In My Chair Snickering
SIMYC	Sorry I missed your call
SIN CITY	Reno NV
SIR	Strike it rich
SIS	Snickering in silence
SIT	Stay in touch
SIYOL	Stay in your own lane
SJW	Social justice warrior
SK8	Skate
SK8NG	Skating
SK8R	Skater
SK8RBOI	Skater Boy
SKL	School
SLAP	Sounds like a plan
SLM	See Last Mail
SMDH	Shaking My Damn Head
SMEXI	Combination of sexy and Mexican used to describe attractive people
SMEXI	Sexy Mexican
SMEXI	Smart and Sexy
SMF	Shaking My F**king Head
SMF	So much fun
SMH	Shaking My Head
SMHID	Scratching my head in disbelief
SMHL	Shaking My Head

	Laughing
SMHOF	Set my heart on fire
SMIM	Send me an Instant Message
SMMFH	Shaking My Mother F**king Head
SMOKEY IN THE BUSH	A speed trap
SMOL	Smiling Out Loud
SMOP	Small Matter of Programming
SMPM	Send me a Private Message
SMRP	Suggested Manufacturer's Retail Price
SMS	Short Message Service
SNAFU	Situation normal all fouled up
SNERT	Snot-nosed egotistical rude teenager
SNS	Social Networking Site
SO	Significant Other
SOAB	Son of a *B*
SOB	Stressed Out Bigtime
SOH	Sense of Humor
SOHF	Sense of Humor Failure
S'OK	It's okay
SOL	S**T Out of Luck
SOL	Sooner or later
SOME1	Someone
SOMY	Sick of me yet?
SOOMB	Stay Out Of My Business

SORG	Straight or Gay?
SORTA	Sort of
SOS	Help
SOS	Same Old Stuff
SOS	Save our souls
SOS	Someone Over Shoulder
SOT	Short of time
SOT	Sticking out tongue
SOTMG	Short of time - must go
SOW	Speaking Of Which
SOWM	Someone with me
SP	Sponsored
SPK	Speak
SPOC	Single point of contact
SPOZ2B	Supposed to be
SPST	Same place same time
SPTO	Spoke to
SQ	Square
SRSLY	Seriously
SRY	Sorry
SS	So sorry
SS	Super Sweet
SSDD	Same Stuff Different Day
SSIF	So stupid it's funny
SSINF	So stupid it's not funny
ST	Stop that
ST&D	Stop texting and drive
ST&D	Stop texting and drive
STAND ON IT	Stand On The Fuel Pedal
STBU	Sucks to be you
STD	Sexually transmitted

	disease
STDNG	Studying
STFU	Shut the *freak* up
STFW	So The F**k What
STN	Spend The Night
STO	Sticking tongue out
STR8	Straight
STS	Smirk To Self
STSP	Same time same place
STTGD	I'm so tired I think I'm Gonna die
STW	Search the Web
SU	Shut Up
SUAC	Shut up and color
SUAC	Stinking up a coffin (i.e. dead)
SUAKM	Shut up and kiss me
SUFID	Screwing Up Face In Disgust
SUITM	See you in the morning
SUL	See you later
SUL	Snooze You Loose
SUP	What's up?
SUX	(It) Sucks
SUYF	Shut up you fool
SW	So What
SWAG	Free stuff and giveaways
SWAG	Scientific wild *a* guess
SWAK	Sealed With A Kiss
SWAK	Sent (or sealed) with a kiss
SWALK	Sealed with a loving kiss

SWIM	See What I Mean
SWL	Screaming With Laughter
SWMBO	She (Wife/Significant Other/Mother) who must be obeyed
SYFM	Shut Your F**king Mouth
SYL	See you later
SYM	Shut Your Mouth
SYS	See You Soon
SYT	Sweet young thing
SYY	Shut your yapper
T Codes	
T:)T	Think happy thoughts
t^t	Tsk-Tsk
T+	Think positive
T4BU	Thanks for being you
TA	Thanks a lot
TABE	Turn a blind eye
TAF	That's All Folks!
TAFN	That's All For Now
TAKING PICTURES	Police Using Radar
TAKS	That's a knee slapper
TAM	Tomorrow a.m.
TANJ	There Ain't No Justice
TANK	Really strong
TANSTAAFL	There Ain't No Such Thing As A Free Lunch
TARITF	There's A Ripple in the

	Force
TARFU	Things Are Really *fouled* Up
TAS	Take a shot
TAU	Thinking about u (you)
TAUMUALU	Thinking about you miss you always love you
TAW	Take a walk
TB	Too Bad
TBA	To Be Announced
TBAG	Taunting a fragged/killed player (online gaming)
TBC	To Be Continued
TBD	To Be Decided
TBFH	To Be F**king Honest
TBH	To Be Honest
TBL	Text back later
TBL8TR	Text back later
TBQFH	To Be Quite F**king Honest
TBQH	To Be Quite Honest
TBS	That's Bull S**t
TBT	Throw Back Thursday
TBYB	Try Before You Buy
TC	Take Care
TC4U	Too cool for you
TCB	Take care of business
TCFU	Too cool for you
TCO	Total Cost of Ownership
TCOY	Take care of yourself
TD	Tower defense (online gaming)

TD2M	Talk dirty to me
TDM	Too Damn Many
TDTM	Talk dirty to me
TF	Too Funny
TFB	Too F**king Bad
TFBS	That's F**king Bull S**t
TFF	Too *freaking* funny
TFFS	That's For F**king Sure
TFG	Thank F**king God
TFN	Till Further Notice
TFN	Total F**king Nightmare
TFS	Thanks for sharing
TFS	That's For Sure
TFS	Three Finger Salute (Ctl-Alt-Del)
TFTF	Thanks For The Follow
TFTHAOT	Thanks For The Help Ahead Of Time
TFTI	Thanks for the invitation
TFTT	Thanks For The Thought
TG	Thank God
TG	Thank goodness
TGAL	Think Globally Act Locally
TGIF	Thank God it's Friday
TGIS	Thank God it's Saturday
THE DOME CITY	Houston TX
THNQ	Thank-you
THNX	Thanks
THROW SOME ROPE	Secure a flatbed load
THT	Think happy thoughts

THX	Thanks
TIA	Thanks In Advance
TIAB	To Infinity And Beyond
TIAD	Tomorrow is another day
TI-AMO	I love you (Italian)
TIC	Tongue In Cheek
TIFS	This Is F**king Stupid
TIL	Today I learned
TILIS	Tell it like it is
TINALO	This Is Not A Legal Opinion
TINWIS	That Is Not What I Said
TIR	Teacher in room
TIS	This Is Stupid
TKS	Thanks
TL	Too long
TLDR	Too long - Didn't Read
TLC	Tender Loving Care
TLK2UL8R	Talk to you later
TM{	Tell me please
TMA	Take my advice
TMB	Text me back
TMB	Tweet me back
TMD	Too Much Drama
TMFD	Too Much F**king Drama
TMFI	Too Much F**king Information
TMHU	Throwing my hands up
TMI	Too Much Information
TMIB	Tell me I'm beautiful
TML	Text me later
TMM	Tell Me More

TMOT	Trust me on this
TMTH	Too much to handle
TMWFI	Take my word for it
TMWIM	Tell Me What It Means
TMYL	Tell me your location
TN	Total Nightmare
TNF	Totally not funny
TNQ	Thank you
TNSTAAFL	There's No Such Thing As A Free Lunch
TNT	Till next time
TNTL	Trying Not To Laugh
TNWIM	That's Not What I Meant
TNWIS	That's Not What I Said
TNX	Thanks
TNXE6	Thanks A Million
TOBAL	There Ought (to) Be A Law
TOBG	This Ought to Be Good
TOJ	Tears of joy
TOMA	Take Over My A$$
TOP	The Original Poster (refers to the one who started this discussion thread)
TOS	Terms of service
TOTBAL	There Ought To Be A Law
TOTES	Totally
TOU	Thinking of U (you)
TOY	Thinking Of You
TOYCL	Turn Your Caps Lock

	OFF
TPM	Tomorrow p.m.
TPTB	The Powers that Be
TQ	Te quiero/ I love you (Spanish)
TRASH TWEETER	A Twitterer who talks trash in his/her posts
TRAVEL AGENT	Dispatcher
TRDMC	Tears Running Down My Cheeks
TRIPLE DIGIT RIDE	Truck That Can Exceed 100 MPH
TS	Totally Stinks
TSFM	Thanks So F**king Much
TSH	Tripping so hard
TSM	Thanks So Much
TSNF	That's so not fair
TSR	Totally Stupid Rules
TSTB	The sooner the better
TTBOMK	To The Best Of My Knowledge
TTC	Text the cell
TTFN	Ta-Ta For Now
TTG	Time To Go
TTKSF	Trying To Keep a Straight Face
TTLY	Totally
TTS	Take The Shot
TTTT	These things take time
TTTT	To Tell The Truth
TTUL	Talk to you later
TTUL8TR	Talk to you later

TTYAFN	Talk to you awhile from now
TTYAT	Talk To You Another Time
TTYAWFN	Talk To You A While From Now
TTYK	To Tell You Kindly
TTYL	Talk To You Later
TTYLIIGAC	Talk To You Later If I Get A Chance
TTYN	Talk To You Never
TTYN	Tell it to your neighbor
TTYS	Talk To You Soon
TTYSTL	Talk To You Sooner Tha n Later
TTYT	Talk To You Tomorrow
TU	Thank you
TUI	Turning you in
TURKEY DAY	Thanksgiving
TURNT	Turn up
TURT	Take your time
TWABE	A young woman (roughly the same as "Babe")
TWABSTINENCE	Describe someone's decision to cut back on their Twitter time because it is preventing them from completing important daily tasks
TWABULOUS	Used to describe a fabulous tweet
TWAFFIC	Twitter traffic
TWALKING	Walking while you Tweet

	using a mobile device
TWART	Twitter Art
TWAT	Female genitalia
TWB4U	That was before you
TWEBAY	Describe selling (or promoting) an eBay item on Twitter
TWEENGLISH	Teenager language only they can understand
TWEEPLE	Twitter users
TWEET	A Twitter update/a post
TWEETAHOLIC	Describe someone who has a problematic addiction to Twitter
TWEETER	An active Twitter user
TWEETERBOXES	Refers to Twitter users who tweet excessively
TWEETORIAL	Describes lecturing on or about Twitter
TWEETRODUCE	A Twitter user introduces one follower to another
TWEETSULT	An insult sent using Twitter
TWEGAL ADVICE	Describes legal advice that is sent on twitter
TWERMINOLOGY	Twitter terminology
TWETTIQUETTE	The Twitter etiquette of acceptable behavior
TWEWBIE	Used to describe someone who is new to Twitter
TWINKEDLIN	Someone who invites their Twitter friends to

	interact with them on LinkedIn
TWISHING	The act of merging Twitter and Phishing usually for wicked reasons
TWITOSPHERE	General term for the Twitter Universe
TWITTCRASTINAT ION	Using Twitter as a form of procrastination
TWITTER	Lets you stay connected through short messages called 'tweets'
TWITTERAGE	Feelings of rage experienced as a result of a Twitter post
TWITTERAPPS	Twitter applications also called Twitter Tools or Twitter Add-Ons
TWITTERATI	Refers to 'A-list' Twitter users
TWITTERER	A person who send tweets on Twitter
TWITTERFLY	A social butterfly on Twitter
TWITTERIFIC	Twitter and Terrific merged used to describe something terrific found on Twitter
TWITTERPATED	Describing the feeling one experiences when messages on Twitter become overwhelming

TWITTERPHORIA	Elation felt when a Twitter user adds a friend and the friend adds them back
TWITTWORKING	Twitterers who use Twitter to network
TWOFT	Total Waste Of F**king Time
TWOT	Total Waste Of Time
TWSS	That's what she said
TX	Thanks
TXT	Text
TY	Thank You
TYCLO	Turn Your CAPS LOCK OFF
TYFC	Thank you for charity (online gaming)
TYFYC	Thank you for your comment
TYS	Told you so
TYSO	Thank you so much
TYT	Take your time
TYVM	Thank You Very Much
U Codes	
U	U
U	You
U2	You Too
UAA	You are an angel
UB	Un-Believable
UCMU	You crack me up

UD	You'd
UDI	Unidentified drinking injury (bruise/scratches/aches)
UDK	You don't know
UDM	You-Da-Man
UDS	Ugly domestic scene
UFB	Un *freaking* believable
UFG	Use F**king Google
UFI	You F**king Idiot
UFN	Until further notice
UFWM	You *freaking* with me?
UG	Use Google
UHGTBSM	You have got to be s#$t*ing me!
UI	You Idiot
UKTR	You know that's right
UL	Upload
ULL	You'll
UN4TUN8	Unfortunate
UNA	Use no acronyms
UNBLEFBLE	Unbelievable
UNCRTN	Uncertain
UNI	Universidad/University - College (Spanish)
UNN	You are not nice
UNO	You know
UNPC	Un/Not politically correct
UOK	(Are) You ok?
UOM	You Owe Me
UOMBT	You Owe Me Big Time
UR	You Are

UR	Your/You're (You Are)
UR2WS4ME	You are too wise for me
URA*	You are a star
URALIMDRMS	You are always in my dream
URAOMM	You are always ion my mind
URH	You are hot (U R Hot)
URK	You rock
URSELF	Yourself
URSKTM	You are so kind to me
URTM	You are the man
URW	You are welcome
USBCA	Until something better comes along
USM	You slay me
USU	Usually
UT	Unreal Tournament (online gaming)
UT2L	You take too long
UTM	You tell me
UV	Unpleasant visual
UW	You will
UWTLF	You with the long face
UYRS	Up yours
V Codes	
V	Very
VAT	Value added tax
VBL	Visible bra line
VBS	Very big smile

VEG	Very evil grin
VFF	Very freaking funny
VFM	Value for money
VGC	Very good condition
VGG	Very good game (online gaming)
VGH	Very good hand (online gaming)
VID	video
VIP	Very important person
VM	Voice Mail
VMT	very many thanks
VN	Very nice
VNH	Very nice hand (online gaming)
VOIP	Voice over Internet Protocol
VPL	Visible panty line
VRY	Very
VS	Vice Versa
VSC	Very soft chuckle
VSF	Very sad face
VWD	Very well done (online gaming)
VWP	Very well played (online gaming)
W Codes	
W/	With
W/B	Welcome back
W/B	Write back

W/E	Whatever
W/O	Without
W@	What?
W00T	We Owned the Other Team
W2G	Way to go
W3	WWW (Web address)
W8	Wait
WAB	We Are Back
WAEF	When All Else Fails
WAFWOT	What A F**king Waste Of Time
WAG	Wild Assed Guess
WAH	Working at home
WAJ	What a jerk
WALLY WORLD	Wal-Mart
WAM	Wait a minute
WAN2	Want to?
WAN2TLK	Want to talk
WANNA	Want to
WAREZ	Pirated (illegally acquired) software
WAS	Wait a second
WAS	Wild *a* guess
WATERMELON 500	Atlanta GA
WAU	What About You
WAU	Who asked you
WAWA	Where are we at?
WAWOT	What A Waste Of Time
WAYD	What Are You Doing?
WAYF	Where are you from?

WB	Welcome Back
WB	Write Back
WBS	Write back soon
WBU	What about you?
WC	Welcome
WC	Who cares
WCA	Who cares anyway
WCUL	will catch you later
WD	Week Day
WDALYIC	Who died and left you in charge
WDD	Whoop Dee Doo
WDFD	Whoop Dee F**king Doo
WDP	Well done partner
WDYK	What do you know?
WDYM	What Did You Mean
WDYMBT	What Do You Mean By That?
WDYS	What did you say
WDYT	What Do You Think
WDYWTTA	What do you want to talk about
WE	Weekend
WE	Whatever
WEBO	Webopedia
WEEBO	A person obsessed with Japanese culture
WEG	Wicked evil grin
W-END	Weekend
WEP	Weapon (online gaming)
WFC	Who F**king Cares?
WFM	Works for me

WFO	Wide F**king Open
WGACA	What do you think?
WH5	Who/What/When/Where/Why
WHATCHA	What are you
WHT	Whatever Happened To
WIBAMU	Well I'll Be A Monkey's Uncle
WIBNI	Wouldn't It Be Nice If
WIGGLE WAGONS	Double OR Triple Trailer Trucks
WIIFM	What's in it for me?
WINDY CITY	Chicago IL
WISP	Winning is so pleasurable
WITP	What's the point?
WITW	What in the world
WIU	Wrap it up
WIYP	What's your point?
WK	Week
WKD	Weekend
WKEND	Weekend
WKF	Well known fact
WL	Whatta loser
WLC	Welcome
WMMOWS	Wash My Mouth Out With Soap
WNOHGB	Where No One Has Gone Before
WNWU	What's new with you
WO	Wide Open
WOA	Work Of Art

WOFTAM	Waste Of F**king Time And Money
WOMBAT	Waste of money brains and time
WOS	Wife over shoulder
WOT	With Out Thinking
WOTAM	Waste Of Time And Money
WOTTM	With Out Thinking Too Much
WOW	World of Warcraft (online gaming)
WOZ	Was (alternate form)
WPYC	Who Pulled Your Chain
WRK	Work
WRT	With Regard To
WRT	With Respect To
WRU	Who are you
WRU@	Where are you at?
WRUD	What Are You Doing
WRUD	What are you doing?
WT	What Time
WT	Without Thinking
WTB	Want to buy (online gaming)
WTBN	Wouldn't That Be Nice
WTC	What the crap
WTF	What the *freak* ?
WTF	What The F***k
WTFH	What The F**king Hell?
WTFIYP	What The F**k Is Your Problem?

WTFS	What The F**king S**t
WTG	Way to Go
WTGP	Want to go private (talk out of public chat area)
WTH	What the heck
WTH	What the hell
WTM	Who's the man?
WTMI	Way Too Much Information
WTR	What's the rush?
WTS	Want to sell? (online gaming)
WTS	What The S**t
WTT	Want to trade? (online gaming)
WTTM	Without Thinking Too Much
WTV	Whatever
WU	What's up?
WUBOL	Will you be on later
WUBU2	What you been up 2
WUCIWUG	What you see is what you get
WUF	Where (are) you from?
WUM	Watch Your Mouth
WUP	What's up?
WUT	What
WUU2	What are you up to?
WUW	What U Want
WUZ	WUZ
WWICU	When will I see you
WWJD	What Would Jesus Do?

WWNC	Will wonders never cease
WWTMI	Way way to much info
WWYC	Write when you can
WWYD	What Would You Do?
WYCM	Will you call me?
WYD	What (are) you doing?
WYFP	What's Your F**king Problem
WYGAM	When you get a minute
WYGISWYPF	What You Get Is What You Pay For
WYHAM	When you have a minute
WYLEI	When you least expect it
WYM	Watch Your Mouth
WYP	What's Your Problem
WYSISWYG	What You See Is What You Get
WYWH	Wish you were here

X Codes

X	Kiss
X!	Typical woman
XCUSE	Excuse
XD	A devilish smile
XD	Laughing
XLNT	Excellent
XLR8	Going Faster
XMAS	Christmas
XME	Excuse Me
XO	Laughing (Wide Open

	Smiley Mouth)
XOXO	Hugs & Kisses
XQZ	Excuse
XYL	Ex-young lady (wife)
XYZ	Examine your zipper

Y Codes

Y	Why
Y/O	Years old
Y?	Why?
Y2K	You're too kind
Y5	Wi-Fi
YAA	Yet another acronym
YAA	You Are Awesome
YAB	You are beautiful
YABA	Yet Another Bloody Acronym
YAFA	You Are F**king Awesome
YAM	Yet another meeting
YAOTM	Yet Another Off-Topic Message
YARD	Trucking Terminal
YARD STICK	Mile Marker
YAUN	Yet Another Unix Nerd
YBFAM	Your Brother From Another Mother
YBI	You Bumbling Idiot
YBIC	Your brother in Christ
YBS	You'll be sorry
YBYSA	You Bet Your Sweet A$$

YCDBWYCID	You can't do business when your computer is down
YCHT	You can have them
YCLIU	You can look it up
YCMU	You crack me up
YCT	Your comment to?
YD	Yesterday
YDK	You don't know
YF	Wife
YFI	You F**king Idiot
YFP	Your F**king Problem
YG	Young gentleman
YGG	You go girl
YGLI	You're Gonna Love It
YGLT	You're Gonna Love This
YGT	You Got This
YGTBK	You've Got To Be Kidding
YGTBKM	You've got to be Kidding me
YGTI	You Get The Idea?
YGWYPF	You Get What You Pay For
YHBT	You have been trolled
YHBW	You have been warned
YHL	You have lost
YIU	Yes I Understand
YIWGP	Yes I Will Go Private
YKW	You know what
YKWIM	You Know What I Mean
YKWYCD	You know what you can

	do
YKYARW	You Know You're A Redneck When
YKYAT	You Know Your Addicted To ...
YL	Young Lady
YM	Young Man
YMMD	You made my day
YMMV	Your mileage may vary
YMW	Your most welcome
YN	Yawn
YNK	You never know
YNTB	Your not the boss
YO	Hey
YOB	Your own boss
YOLO	You Only Live Once
YOM	You Owe Me
YOYO	You're On Your Own
YP	Your Problem
YQW	Your quite welcome
YR	Yeah right
YR	Year
YR	Your
YRA	You Are Awesome
YRYOCC	You're running your own cuckoo clock
YSIC	Your sister in Christ
YSUL	You Snooze You Loose
YSYD	Yeah sure you do
YT	You there?
YTB	You're the best
YTG	You're the greatest

YTTL	You take too long
YUP	Yes
YUP	Yes - Understood (now) proceed
YVW	You're very welcome
YW	You're welcome
YWHNB	Yes - We have no bananas
YWHOL	Yelling Woo-Hoo out loud
YWSYLS	You win some - you lose some
YYSSW	Yeah yeah sure sure whatever
Z Codes	
Z	Zero
Z%	Zoo
ZH	Sleeping Hour
ZOMG	Oh My God (World of Warcraft)
ZOT	Zero tolerance
ZTWITT	To tweet extremely fast
ZUP	What's up?
ZZZZZ	Dormir/Sleeping

147

Codes, Acronyms, Abbreviations, and Phrases: The shorthand of the digital age

(Alphabetical by Description)

Description	Code
Special Descriptions	
(Means) Read Line above	^^
(Means) Read Message above	^^
(Are) You ok?	UOK
(be)Cause	CUZ
(ET) Phone Home	38
(I have a) question for you	Q4U
(It) Sucks	SUX
(Promise) On my soul	OMS
(w)Hole 'nother level	HNL
Freak all you	FAY
Freak 'em if they can't take a joke	FEITCTAJ
Freak I'm funny	FIF
Freak My Life	FML
Freak off and die	FOAD
Freak you	FU
Freaked if I know	FIIK
24/7 (All day - every day!)	247

2-Good-4-U	224
55 Miles Per Hour	DOUBLE NICKEL
9 foot whip antenna	BIG MAMA

A Descriptions

An antenna that really sways	BALLET DANCER
A beginner - Someone who is bad at (online) games	NOOB
A Big F**king Waste Of Time	ABFWOT
A Big Waste Of Time	ABWOT
A cab with no trailer attached	BOB TAIL
A Car With It's Wheels In The Air	GREASY SIDE UP
A CB addict	APPLE
A CB rig	BEAST
A Completely Obsessive Really Nutty Person	ACORNP
A crowded channel	BAD SCENE
A devilish smile	XD
A fresh pair of eyes	AFPOE
A full blown bear (state trooper)	BIG BEAR
A hash tag (hashtag) is a way of organizing your updates	HASH TAG
A hashtag letting others know you'd like to exchange guest blog posts	#BEMYGUEST
A hot tweet - usually a popular trending topic on Twitter	BEETWEET
A Kenworth T-600 (nicknamed	AARDVARK

'the anteater')	
A Lot	ALT
A loud or strong signal	BLEW MY DOORS OFF
A misleading tweet similar to a crank phone call	CRANK TWEET
A new CB rig	BLESSED EVENT
A new Twittter user	NEWEETER
A not-so-formal name for a good neighbor	BUBBA
A penis (U.S. Slang)	DORK
A person obsessed with Japanese culture	WEEBO
A person who send tweets on Twitter	TWITTERER
A photo that is taken of oneself for social media sharing	SELFIE
A phrase used in online chat to annoy those involved	DEEZ NUTZ
A Plain Freight Trailer With NO Refrigerator	DRY BOX
A police car with its lights on	ADVERTISING
A Police plane or helicopter	ASTRONAUT
A quick howdy to you!	485
A Ripple In The Force	ARITF
A second person on a single Twitter account	CO-TWITTERER
A self-proclaimed CB expert	BOAST TOASTIE
A shortened version of details	DEETS
A skank; a slut; a person (male or female) who would f**k	HOE

anything	
A social butterfly on Twitter	TWITTERFLY
A socially inept person	DORK
A speed trap	BEAR IN THE GRASS
A speed trap	SMOKEY IN THE BUSH
A substitute for F**KING	FREAKIN
A third-party CBer trying to breakup communication between two other stations by keying his microphone or playing sounds	BUTTON PUSHER
A truck hauling cars	PARKING LOT
A Truck Who Drags Up a Hill And Flies Down	DRAGON FLY
A Tweet send from a Blackberry device	BBERRYTWEET
A tweet sent from a restaurant drive-thru	DRIVE THRU TWEET
A tweet that contains useful knowledge sent out daily	DAILY TWITAMIN
A tweet that you later regret having sent	MISTWEET
A Twitter System failure image	FAIL WHALE
A Twitter update directed as a reply	@REPLY
A Twitter update/a post	TWEET
A Twitter user introduces one follower to another	TWEETRODUCE
A Twitterer who adds many friends within a short time period	FRIENDAPALOOZA

A Twitterer who talks trash in his/her posts	TRASH TWEETER
A type of blog that lets users publish short text updates	MICROBLOG
A user who talks about himself on Twitter	EGOTWISTICAL
A usually intelligent person who is socially awkward and does not fit in	GEEK
A Word To The Wise	AWTTW
A young woman (roughly the same as "Babe")	TWABE
A$$Hat - Somebody with the head so far up their a$$ they could use it as a hat	AH
Abbreviation	ABBR
About	ABT
About	BOUT
About F**king Time	AFT
About Time	AT
About To	ABT2
Absent With Out Leave	AWOL
Accept	ACPT
Acceptable content	AC
Accident	ACDNT
Acknowledge	ACK
Acquisition	ACQSTN
Acronym Free Zone	AFZ
Acronym rich environment	ARE
Active Duty	AD
Actually Laughing Out Loud	ALOL
Addicted To Texting	A2T

Address	ADD
Address	ADDY
Address	ADR
Adios	AD
Adios Amigo	ADA
Adios/Goodbye	A2
Adios/Goodbye	DEW
Adjust your attitude	600
Administrator	ADMIN
Administrator (Government)	ADMINR
Administrator Over Shoulder	AOS
Administrators On-Line	A-OLs
Administrators On-Line (may be monitoring)	AOL
Adorable	DORBS
Adult Disease	AD
Adult in the room	AITR
Affiliated League of Emergency Radio Teams	ALERT
Affirmative/Yes	124
After while crocodile	AWC
Age - Sex - Location - Photo	ASLP
Age - Sex - Location	ASL
Age - Sex - Location - Availability	ASLA
Age of majority	AOM
Age of Mythology (online gaming)	AOM
Age/sex/location	A/S/L
Aggression factor (online gaming)	AF
Agility (online gaming)	AGI

Agree To Disagree	A2D
Agreement In Principle	AIP
Airhead	000
Airport	300
Alcoholics Anonymous	AA
Alive and kicking	AAK
Alive and smiling	AAS
All buggered up	ABU
All concerned	ALCON
All Day	AD
All Day Long	ADL
All done - bye-bye	ADBB
All F**ked Up	AFU
All F**king Day	AFD
All For Now	AFN
All my best wishes	AMBW
All My Love	AML
All of the above	AOTA
All Points Bulletin	APB
All praise and credit	APAC
All Right	ALR
All The Best	ATB
All the stars in the sky	ATSITS
All The Time	ATT
All The Way	ATW
All your base are belong to us (online gaming)	AYBABTU
Along The Same Line	ATSL
Already been chewed	ABC
Already been done	ABD
Alright	AIGHT
Also Known As	AKA

ALT / CONTROL / DELETE	ACD
Always	6
Always & forever	637
Always A Pleasure	AAP
Always And Forever	AAF
Always At The Keyboard	AATK
Always Dependable (but) Politically Incorrect	ADPIC
Always Here For You	AHFY
Always In My Prayers	AIMP
Always On My Mind	AOMM
Amarillo TX	BIG A
Amazing	AMAZN
Ambivalent	:-|
Ambulance	MEAT-WAGON
America On Line	AOL
America's Next Top Model	ANTM
An 18 Wheeler	BIG RIG
An 18 wheeler	BIG TRUCK
An active Twitter user	TWEETER
An adventurous Twitterer	ADVENTURIT TER
An incompetent/foolish/stupid person	DOOFUS
An insult sent using Twitter	TWEETSULT
An intermittent tone signal	BEER TONE
An old radio that is unrepairable	BOAT ANCHOR
An intelligent but single-minded person obsessed with a nonsocial hobby or pursu	NERD

it	
Anarchy Online (online gaming)	AO
And	&&
And	N
And I am a money's uncle	AIAMU
And Now For A Word From Our Sponsor	ANFAWFOS
And Now For Something Completely Different	ANFSCD
And so it goes	ASIG
And You're Telling Me This Because	AYTMTB
Angel	AGL
Angel on your pillow	AOYP
Angelic	O:-)
Angels Forever - Forever Angels	AFFA
Angry	> > :-(
Angry and swearing	:@
Anno Domini (Year of Our Lord)	AD
Another Cluster F**k	ACF
Another Day Another Dollar	ADAD
Another Day In Hell	ADIH
Another Day In Paradise	ADIP
Another F**king Growth Opportunity	AFGO
Another Growth Opportunity	AGO
Another Subject	AS
Answer back	BRING IT BACK
Antivirus	AV
Any	NE

Any Day Now	ADN
Any F**king Day Now	AFDN
Any Thing You Say	ATYS
Anyhow	NEHOW
Anymore	NEMORE
Anyone	AN1
Anyone	NE1
Anyone can come	ACC
Anyone for KFC?	NE14KFC?
Anytime - Anywhere - Anyplace	A3
Anyway For What It's Worth	AFWW
Applause	_/_
Application	APP
Appreciate	APR
April Fools	AF
April Fools Joke	AFJ
Archive (compressed files)	ARC
Are	R
Are u (you) there?	RUT
Are u free	RUFRE
Are We Going To Have To Go Through This Again?	AWGTHTGTTA
Are we having fun yet?	435
Are We Having Fun Yet?	AWHFY
Are We Square	RWSQ
Are We There Yet	AWTY
Are You Serious	AYS
Are you booked?	5-0
Are you busy	QRL
Are You Coming	RYC
Are you done yet?	AYDY
Are You F**king Kidding Me	RUFKM

Are You F**king Kidding Me?	AYFKM
Are You F**king Serious	AYFS
Are You For Real	RUFR
Are You Kidding Me	RUKM
Are You Kidding Me?	AYKM
Are you male or female?	RUMOF
Are You OK?	RUOK
Are you ready to say goodbye?	BYE?
Are You Serious	RUS
Are you single?	RYS
Are you stupid or something?	AYSOS
Are you there?	AYT
Are you there?	R U THERE
Are you vertical?	AYV
Are you?	RU
Area effect (online gaming)	AE
Area of effect (online game)	AOE
Argument	ARG
Artificial Intelligence	AI
As *Freak*	AF
As a friend	AAF
As a matter of fact	AAF
As A Matter Of Fact	AAMOF
As a matter of fact	AMOF
As A Matter Of Fact	ASMOF
As A Matter Of Interest	AAMOI
As above	AA
As always - your friend	AAYF
As early as possible	AEAP
As far as I am aware	AFAIAA
As Far As I Am Concerned	AFAIAC
As Far As I Can Tell	AFAICT

As Far as I Know	AFAIK
As Far As I Remember	AFAIR
As far as I understand it	AFAIUI
As Far As You Know	AFAYK
As Fast As Possible	AFAP
As I remember	AIR
As I Said Before	AISB
As I See It	AISI
As I Understand It	AIUI
As If	AF
As It Happens	AIH
As It Should Be	AISB
As Long As Possible	ALAP
As Much As I Can Recall	AMAICR
As Much as I Recall	AMAIR
As much as possible	AMAP
As quick (or quiet) as possible	AQAP
As Simple As That	ASAT
As Soon As F**king Possible	ASAFP
As Soon As Possible	ASAP
As Soon As You Get This	ASAYGT
As Well As	AWA
As You Know	AYK
As You Well Know	AYWK
As You Were	AYW
As You Wish	AYW
Asian	AZN
Ask about	AA
Ask Me Something	AMS
Asleep	I-i
Asleep At Keyboard	AAK
Associate Degree	AD

Associate Director	AD
At	@
At any rate	AAR
At Home	AH
At my place	318
At my work	319
At The End Of The Day	@TEOTD
At the end of the day	ATEOTD
At the job site	314
At the place we talked about	322
At this moment	ATM
At What Time	AWT
At your earliest convenience	AYEC
At Your Own Risk	AYOR
At your terminal	AYT
Ate	8
Atlanta GA	WATERMELO N 500
Audio Frequency	AF
Audio Visual	AVID
Aujourd'hui/Today	AUJ
Author's note	A/N
Automatic noise limiter	ANL
Available On Cell	AOC
Away from computer	AFC
Away from Keyboard	AFK
Awesome	AWESO
Awesome	AZM
Awesome	BODACIOUS

B Descriptions	
Babe or baby	BAE
baby	BB
Back	B
Back	BK
Back At Keyboard	BAK
Back at ya	BAY
Back In The Saddle	BITS
Back Of The Book	BOTB
Back Off	BO
Back off *buddy*	BOB
Back Off You Dipstick	BOYDS
Back On Topic	BOT
Back real soon	BRS
Back The H*LL Off	BTHO
Back To Computer	BAC
Back to keyboard	B2K
Back to keyboard	BTK
Back to topic	BTT
Back to work	B2W
Background - A request for more information	BGD
Background (personal information request)	B/G
Bacon and Mushrooms	B&M
Bad A$$	BA
Bad A$$ Chick	BAC
Bad A$$ Mother F**ker	BAMF
Bad A$$ Trick	BAT
Bad News	BN
Bad News In Box	BNIB
Bad reception	10-1

Bait (person being teased)	B8
Bait (under-aged person as in 'jail bait')	B8
Band aide	(::():::)
Bank	302
Banned	B&
Banned	BND
Base station with many antennas strung up in the air	ANTENNA FARM
Based on my experience	BME
Based On My Experience	BOME
Basic	BSC
Bat you on (the) head	BYOH
Bath Room Break	BRB
Bathroom	BR
Bathroom break	BIO
Batteries Not Included	BNI
Battlefield 2 (online gaming)	BF2
B-day-boy	8-084-804
Be	B
Be aware of	BAO
Be back	BB
Be Back in a Bit	BBIAB
Be Back In A Few	BBIAF
Be Back In A Minute	BBIAM
Be back in a sec	BBIAS
Be Back Later	BBL
Be Back Much Later	BBML
Be Back Shortly	BBS
Be Back Tomorrow	BBT
Be Back Whenever	BBW
Be cool	BC

Be gentle with me	BGWM
Be Good	22
Be Home At	BH@
Be Home Late	BHL8
Be Home Soon	BHS
Be Kool	BK
Be my guest	BYG
Be On Later	BOL
Be on the look out	BOLO
Be Right Back	BRB
Be right back - nature calls	BRNC
Be right back *babe*	BRBB
Be right here	BRH
Be right there	BRT
Be Safe	BS
Be Seeing You	BCNU
Be That As It May	BTAIM
Be There Or Be Dead	BTOBD
Be There Or Be Square	BTOBS
Be Well	BW
Be With Me	15243
Be your own boss	BYOB
Beats The Hell Out Of Me	BTHOOM
Beats the Sh*t Out Of Me	BTSOOM
Beaucoup/A lot	BCP
Beautiful	90
Bebe	8383
Bebe/Baby	BB
Bebi/Baby (Spanish)	BB
Because	B/C
Because	BC
Because	BCAS

Because	BCOS
because	BCOZ
Because	BCUZ
Because	BK
Because	COZ
Been There - Done That	BTDT
Beer in - Beer out	BIBO
Before	B4
Before anyone else	BAE
Before I Forget	BIF
Before now	B4N
Before you came along	BYCA
Before You Forget	BYF
Behind	BHD
Behind you or to the rear	BACK DOOR
Believe it or not	BION
Belly laugh	BL
Below Average Mentality	BAM
Bend Over Here It Comes Again	BOHICA
Bending over smacking my knee laughing	BOSMKL
Benefit Of The Doubt	BOTD
Besitos/Kisses	BSS
Best and final offer	BAFO
Best F**king Friends Forever	BFFF
Best friend	BF
Best friend at work	BFAW
Best friend for now	BFFN
Best friend forever for life	BFF4LIFE
Best friend(s) forever and ever	BFFAE
Best Friends For Life	BFFL

Best friends for life no matter what	BFFLNMW
Best friends forever	477
Best Friends Forever	BFF
Best Guy Friend	BGF
Best in slot (online gaming)	BIS
Best known as	BKA
Best of luck to you today	390
Best Regards	BR
Best wishes	ALL THE GOOD NUMBERS
Better Half	BH
Better Late Than Never	BLTN
Better luck next time	BLNT
Better Safe Than Sorry	BSTS
Better shut up	BSU
Better You Than Me	BYTM
Between	BTW
Between	BTWN
Between me and you	BM&Y
Between technologies	BT
Between You And I	BUAI
Beyond that	BOT
Bien Sur/Of Course	B1SUR
Big Deal	BD
Big A$$' Smile	BAS
Big bad challenge	BBC
Big Beautiful Women	BBW
Big Black Women	BBW
Big Brother	BB
Big 'butt' smile	BAS

Big Crush On	BCO
Big crush on you	BCOY
Big darn number	BDN
Big Evil Grin	BEG
Big F**king bitch	BFB
Big F**king Deal	BFD
Big F**king Gun	BFG
Big F**king Idiot	BFI
Big Freakin' Deal	BFD
Big Freakin' Rock	BFR
Big Frickin Deal	BFD
Big Friendly Giant	BFG
Big Grin	BG
Big Idiot	BI
Big person little mind	BPLM
Big Red Switch	BRS
Big Road (major highway)	BR
Big smile	:D
Big Time Operator	BTO
Big Wide Grin	BWG
Big freaking grin	BFG
Bind on equip (online gaming)	BOE
Bind on pickup (online gaming)	BOP
Birmingham Alabama	B TOWN
Birthday	BDAY
Birthday	B-DAY
Bi-sexual	BI
Bitch	606
Bitching and Moaning	B&M
Bite Me	BM
Bite this	BT
Black and white	B&W

Black Friday	BF
Blind courtesy copy	BCC
Blonde With Brunette Roots	BWBR
Blood Elf (online gaming)	BELF
Bloody Hell	BH
Blow It Out Your A$$	BIOYA
Blow it out your nose	BIOYN
Blow Job/Blowjob: A sex act	BJ
Blow My Brains Out	BMBO
Blowing a kiss	:-{}
Blue Screen Of Death	BSOD
Body Off Baywatch - Face Off Crime watch	BOBFOC
Boite aux lettres/Mailbox	BAL
Bonus Question	BQ
Boo	800
Booty call	BTYCL
Bored	\-O
Bored	BRD
Bored Out Of My Skull	BOOMS
Boring Beyond Belief	BBB
Boss is back	BIB
Boss is watching	B9
Boss Over Shoulder	BOS
Boston MA	BEAN TOWN
Boy Am I Confused	BMIC
Boy Friend	BF
Boyfriend	B/F
Boyfriend	BOYF
Boy-Girl Relationship	BGR
Boys' Night Out	BNO
Brain Dead User	BDU

Brain Fart	BF
Brain Free User	BFU
Brains By Mattel	BBM
Brat Over Shoulder	BOS
Breathing a Sigh Of Relief	BASOR
Brick and Mortar	B&M
Bring your own beer	BYOB
Bring Your Own Booze	BYOB
Bring Your Own Bottle	BYOB
Bring your own computer	BYOC
Bring your own device	BYOD
Bring Your Own Mac	BYOM
Bring your own paint (paintball)	BYOP
Brother (Mandarin Chinese)	GG
Brother-In-Law	BIL
Buddy List	B/L
Buddy List	BL
Buddy of mine	BOM
Bull F**king S**t	BFS
Bulls**t	BS
Bummed out	:-C
Burn in hell	BIH
Burnt Beyond Repair	BBR
Bursting With Laughter	BWL
Business as usual	BAU
Business-to-business	B2B
Business-to-consumer	B2C
Bust A Move	BAM
Busted	222
Busted	BSTD
Busting a gut	BAG
Busting my gut with laughter	BYGWL

Busy	BZ
But	315
But I Still Love You	BISLY
But in the meantime	BITMT
But Not Really	BNR
But now something completely different	BNSCD
But of course	BOC
But seriously folks	BSF
But Then Again	BTA
But Wait There's More	BWTM
But What Do I Know	DWDIK
But You Knew That	BYKT
Butt F**king Egypt	BFE
Butt F**king Ugly	BFU
Butt In Chair	BIC
Butt On Chair	BOC
Butt Ugly	BU
Buy One - Get One (free or at discount)	BOGO
Buzz Word Quotient	BWQ
By The By	BTB
By The F**king Way	BTFW
By The Way	BTW
By the way I think I am in love with you	BTWITIAILWU
Bye Bye	BB
Bye Bye	BUBHYE
Bye Bye	BUBI
Bye Bye Baby	BBB
Bye Bye For Now	BBFN
Bye For Now	B4N

Bye For Now	BFN
Bye-bye (Mandarin Chinese)	88
Bye-bye now	BBN

C Descriptions

C Plus Plus	CPP
Call	103
Call back now	343
Call Back Please	346
Call For Votes	CFV
Call Me	41
Call me	CM
Call Me Back	CMB
Call Me Later	425
Call me later	CML
Call Me Now	423
Call me tomorrow	428
Call me tonight	426
Call me whenever	428
Call Of Duty	COD
Call The Cell	CTC
Call you later	CYL
Calling for you	CFY
Camara/Camera	CAM
Can	CN
Can I See You	CICU
Can of coke	|c|
Can of Pepsi	|p|
Cancel that	105
Can't Add - Doesn't Even Try	CADET
Can't Be Bothered	CBB

Can't Be F**king Bothered	CBFB
Can't F**king Wait	CFW
Can't remember a freaking thing	CRAFT
Can't Remember S**t	CRS
Can't remember stuff	CRS
Can't Remember The Acronym	CRTA
Can't stop laughing	CSL
Can't stop talking	:( )
Can't talk	CT
Can't Talk Now	CTN
Can't Talk Now	CTN
Can't Wait	CW
Can't win for losing	CWFL
Car	FOUR WHEELER
Car problems	219
Car Too Close To Bumper	BUMPER STICKER
Car/ Truck	404
Care for a secret?	CFAS
Care to chat	c2c
Care to chat	CTC
Cassette tape	|*-*|
Catch Ya On The Flip Side	CYOTFS
Catch You Later	CUL
Catch You Later	CUL8R
Cause	CS
cause (Because)	COS
CB Channel 19	SESAME STREET
CBer who is "ALL Mouth and	ALLIGATOR

NO Ears"	RADIO
Cell phone	CFN
Cell phone	CP
Center	CTR
Center Median Strip	COMEDIAN
Change	106
Change the subject	CTS
Change your mind	CYM
Change(d) my mind	CMM
Changed and is now weaker (online gaming)	NERF
Charlotte NC	QUEEN CITY
Chat break	CB
Chat Lingo	CHINGO
Chat post (or continue in IM)	CP
Chat room	CR
Chat With You Later	CWYL
Chat Word Dictionary	CWD
Chattanooga TN	CHOO-CHOO
Check	CHK
Check Face Book	CFB
Check This Out	CTO
Check your email	CYM
Check your e-mail	CYE
Check your mail	265
Check your settings	CYS
Checking My email	CME
Cheer up!	440
Chicago IL	WINDY CITY
Chicks	CHIX
Chicks	CHX
Christmas	XMAS

Chuckle & grin	C&G
Chuckle/Snicker/Grin	CSG
Ciao For Now	C4N
City of Heroes (online gaming)	COH
City Police	CITY KITTY
Clap	<>
Class	KLS
Click	CLK
Click back	CKBK
Close of Business	COB
Close your eyes partner (online gaming)	CYEP
Clowning	:*)
Code 9 - Parents or Supervisor around	CD9
Code Of Conduct	COC
Coffee break	CB
Coffee in - Coffee out	CICO
Combination of sexy and Mexican used to describe attractive people	SMEXI
Come back later	CBl
Come back soon	CBS
Come get me	211
Come here	CH
Come home by (time)	101
Come on	CMON
Come Over	108
Come right back	CRB
Complete Waste Of Time	CWOT
Completely F**king Useless	CFU
Completely useless	CU

Computer	COMP
Computer program	PROGGY
Computer programmer	PROGMR
Conference or Company	CO
Congratulations	GRATZ
Congratulations!	11111111
Consider It Done	CID
Contact me to follow up - Hit Me Up	HMU
Continued Next Post	CNP
Control + Alt + Delete	CAD
Conversation	CONV
Conversation	CONVO
Conversation	QSO
Cool	CUL
Cool	KEWL
Cool	KL
Cool	KWL
Cool As A Cucumber	CAC
Cool like you	CLU
Cool like you	KLU
Coolest Person Ever	CPE
Cop	BLACK'N WHITE
Cop with CB in his car	BLACK'N WHITE CBER
Copy and Paste	C&P
Correct Me If I'm Wrong	CMIIW
Correct time	10-38
Correction	CX
Could	CLD
Counter-Strike Source (online	CSS

gaming)	
Course Of Action	COA
Courtesy copy	CC
Cousin	CUZ
Cousin	CUZO
Cousin	CUZSIN
Cover my *a* partner (online gaming)	CMAP
Cover Your A$$	CYA
Cover Your Own A$$	CYOA
Cracking the *heck* up	CTHU
Cracking the F**k Up	CTFU
Crawling under the table laughing	CUTTL
Crazy	CRZ
Crazy Bastard	CB
Crazy Bitch	CB
Create	CR8
Create	CRE8
Critical hit (online gaming)	CRIT
Cross post	C/P
Crying	:'
Crying In Disgrace	CID
Crying like a baby	CLAB
Crying Out Loud	COL
Crying really big tears	CRBT
Crying sadly	:'-(
Crying with joy	:'-)
Crying your eyes out (Mandarin Chinese)	55555
Cuando/When	CDO
Cup (coffee/tea)	_/7

Cut and Paste	KP
Cut the crap	CTC
Cutie	QT
Cutie pie	CTP
Cutie pie	QTPI

D Descriptions

D.O.T./D.M.V. enforcement man	DIESEL COP
D'accord/OK	DAC
Dallas TX	BIG D
Damage per second (online gaming)	DPS
Damned If I Know	DIIK
Dance together	DTG
Dang Typos	DT
Dark Age of Camelot (online gaming)	DAOC
Darling	DRLNG
Darling Husband (usually used with a hint of sarcasm)	DH
Darling Spouse (usually used with at least a hint of sarcasm)	DS
Darling Wife (usually used with at least a hint of sarcasm)	DW
Darn You	DU
Darned if I know	DIIK
Date	D8
Date Of Birth	DOB
Daughter of Eve	DOE
Daughter-In-Law	DIL

Day Be Fore (before)	DB4
Day of Week	DOW
Day of Year	DOY
Daycare	303
Days	DAIZ
Dead	DED
Dead *freaking* last (online gaming)	DFL
Dead F**king Last	DFL
Dead Last	DL
Dead on Arrival	DOA
Dear (or Darling) daughter	DD
Dear (or Darling) daughter	DEGT
Dear (or Darling) son	DS
Dedos/Fingers (Spanish)	D2
Deer Crossing	ANTLER ALLEY
Define the relationship	DTR
Delicious/Yummy	:-9
Deliver to	108
Descends/Get down	D100
Describe a tweet made then deleted	DETWEET
Describe a tweet that has been sent by a drunk user	DWEET
Describe selling (or promoting) an eBay item on Twitter	TWEBAY
Describe someone who has a problematic addiction to Twitter	TWEETAHOLIC
Describe someone's decision to cut back on their Twitter time because it is preventing them from completing important daily	TWABSTINENCE

tasks	
Describes an attraction between two users	ATTWACTION
Describes lecturing on or about Twitter	TWEETORIAL
Describes legal advice that is sent on twitter	TWEGAL ADVICE
Describes someone who is addicted to Twitter	ATTWICTED
Describing the feeling one experiences when messages on Twitter become overwhelming	TWITTERPAT ED
Desole/I'm Sorry	DSL
Details	DTLS
Detroit MI	MOTOR CITY
Deviate	DV8
Devilish	> :-(
Devilish wink	>;->
Dictionary	DXNRY
Did I say?	DIS
Did I tell you I'm distressed?	DITYID
Did You Find It	DYFI
Did you see that	DUCT
Did You Talk To Her/him	DYTTH
Did You Understand That	DYUT
Didn't	DINT
Didn't read	DR
Didn't You Know	DUK
Didn't You Know That	DYKT
Die in a fire	DIAF
Diesel Fuel	MOTION

	LOTION
Different	DIFF
Different Day - Same Sh**	DDSS
Different Day - Same Stuff	DDSS
Dificil/Difficult	DFCL
Dinner	DNR
Dinosaur hugs (used to show support)	DHU
Direct message	DM
Direct Message lets you send a private message to a person	DM
Direct message (Twitter slang)	DM
Directional Antenna	BEAM
Dirty Hippy	DH
Dirty F**king Hippy	DFH
Dirty F**king Redneck	DFR
Dirty Old Man	DOM
Dirty Redneck	DR
Disconnect	DC
Disconnected	D/CED
Disconnected	DCED
Dispatcher	TRAVEL AGENT
Display Picture (Yahoo Messenger Chat)	DP
Ditto to your last page	445
Divorced white female	DWF
Divorced white male	DWM
Do I know You	DIKU
Do I Know You	DIKY
Do I Know You?	DIKU?
Do I look like I give a *freak*?	DILLIGAF

Do I Look Like I Give A Damn?	DILLIGAD
Do I Look Like I Give A F**k	DILLIGAF
Do I look like i give a sugar?	DILLIGAS
Do It Your Dang Self	DIYD
Do It Yourself	DIY
Do Me	DM
Do Not Disturb	DND
Do Not F**king Disturb	DNFD
Do Not Feed The Trolls	DNFTT
Do The Right Thing	DTRT
Do What I Mean - Correctly!	DWIMC
Do What I Mean Not What I Say	DWIMNWIS
Do you hear me	QRK
Do You Know	DYK
Do you know what you are talking about?	DYNWUTB
Do you remember?	DUR
Do your own research (common stock market chat slang)	DYOR
Doctors Office	308
Document	DOC
Does	DUZ
Does My Radio Work?	RADIO CK
Does not compute (I do not understand)	DNC
Doesn't	DUZNT
Doesn't Add Up	DAU
Doesn't matter	DM
Doing business as	DBA
Don't go anywhere	DGA

Don't Know	DK
Donde/Where	DND
Don't	DNT
Don't	DONT
Don't Be Gay	DBG
Don't be lolly-gagging around	465
Don't believe everything you read	DBEYR
Don't Bug Me Now	DBMN
Don't Call Me	064
Don't Care	DC
Don't come	DC
Don't disturb me	DDM
Don't even f**king go there	DEFGT
Don't even go there	DEGT
Don't F**king Care	DFC
Don't F**king Kill Me	DFKM
Don't F**king Know Don't F**king Care	DFKDFC
Don't Forget To Be Awesome	DFTBA
Don't give a *freak*	DGAF
Don't give a care	DGAC
Don't go there	DGT
Don't go there girlfriend	DGTG
Don't go there my friend	DGTMF
Don't Have A Clue	DHAC
Don't Have A F**king Clue	DHAFC
Don't Hold Your Breath	DHYB
Don't Kill Me	DKM
Don't know	DUNNO
Don't Know - Don't Care	DKDC
Don't leave	605

Don't let (the) bed bugs bite	DLBBB
Don't Let The Bed Bugs Bite	DLTBBB
Don't Let Them Catch You	DLTCU
Don't lie to me	DLTM
Don't make me come get you	455
Don't Mention It	DMI
Don't Mess With Me	DMWM
Don't mess yourself	DMY
Don't Over Engineer It	DOEI
Don't Quit Your Day Job	DQYDJ
Don't quote me on this	DQMOT
Don't Really Care	DRC
Don't Really Know	DRK
Don't Sweat It	DSI
Don't text back	DTB
Don't think so	DTS
Don't touch that dial	DTTD
Don't Understand	DU
Don't Worry	DW
Don't You Dare	DYD
Don't you just hate it when...?	DYJHIW
Dormir/Sleeping	ZZZZZ
Double Nickel (55 MPH speed limit)	DN
Double OR Triple Trailer Trucks	WIGGLE WAGONS
Down	DN
Down for sex?	D46?
Down In The Gutter	DITG
Down Load	DL
Down Low	DL
Down Low	DLO

Download	D/L
Download	DL
Downloaded	D/LD
Downloading	D/LG
Dragon kill points (online gaming)	DKP
Drinking glass	( )
Drive An Empty Truck and Trailer To Get A Load Elsewhere	DEADHEAD
Driver	HAND
Driver Has Finished Talking	BACK OUT
Driving Tractor With NO Trailer Attached	BOBTAIL
Drop dead gorgeous	DDG
Drugs or prescriptions	RX
Drunk	""""8*#"
Drunk	:*)
Drycleaners	305
Duck And Cover	DAC
Dude	D00D
Dude - No Offense	DNO
Dude Man - No Offense	DMNO
Dude you fascinate me	DYFM
Due diligence	DD
Dumb A$$	DA
Dumb A$$ Hole	DAH
Dumb A$$ Question	DAQ
Dumb a** loser	DAL
Dumb Hippy	DH
Dumb Question Of The Day	DQOTD
Dumb Redneck	DR

Dungeon Master (online gaming)	DM
Duplicate	DUPE
Durham NC	BULL CITY

E Descriptions

Each	EA
Ear to ear grin	E2EG
Easier	EZR
Easiest	EZEST
Easy	EZ
Easy	EZY
Easy as one - two - three	E123
Eat *S* and die!	ESAD
Eat it	EI
Eat Me	32
Eating at keyboard	EAK
Eavesdropping on social media without participating	LERKR
Ecstasy	E
Edited to add	ETA
Editing in progress	EIP
Effects	FX
Effort	EF4T
Eighteen wheeler	BUCKET OF BOLTS
Elation felt when a Twitter user adds a friend and the friend adds them back	TWITTERPHO RIA
Elite	1337
E-mail	EM

E-mail address	EMA
E-mail message	EMSG
Emailing while intoxicated	EWI
Embarrassed/Embarrassing	EMBAR
Emergency	10-1
Emergency	911
Emergency - All stations stand by	10-33
Emoticons	EMCONS
Emotion	EMO
En tout cas/In any case	ENTK
End of Business	EOB
End of Business Day	EOBD
End Of Day	EOD
End of discussion	EOD
End of file	EOF
End of lecture	EOL
End of Life	EOL
End of Message	73
End of message	EOM
End of show	EOS
End of the world	EOTW
End of thread	EOT
End of transmission	EOT
Enemy (online gaming)	E
Enfadado/Angry	GRRR
Engage Brain Before Starting Mouth	EBBSM
Enough	ENUF
Enough	ENUFF
Enough said	ES
Envy	NV

Epic Failure	EPIF
Equivalent	EQV
Erase display	ED
Erase screen	ES
Eres tz/Are You (Spanish)	ERS2
Erotic Role-Play (online gaming)	ERP
Error between keyboard and chair	EBKAC
Estimated time (of) arrival	ETA
Ever	EVA
Ever Quest (online gaming)	EQ
Every	EVRY
Everyone	E1
Everyone	ER1
Everyone	EVERY1
Everyone	EVR1
Everyone	EVRY1
Everything's O.K.	104
Everything's O.K.	10-4
Evil Grin	<EG>
Evil grin	EG
Evil wicked grin (teasing - in fun)	EWG
Evolution	EVO
Exaggerating - Telling of tall tails	BLOWING SMOKE
Examine your zipper	XYZ
Excellent	XLNT
Excitable yet calm	EYC
Excuse	XCUSE
Excuse	XQZ

Excuse Me	XME
Excuse me for butting in	EMFBI
Excuse me for jumping in	EMFJI
Exhausted - Wiped out	:-6
Expressway / Freeway	BIG SLAB
Extended Three Letter Acronym	ETLA
Extra life (online gaming)	1UP
Extra Lights On A Truck	CHICKEN LIGHTS
Ex-young lady (wife)	XYL

F Descriptions

F**k My F**king Life	FMF
F**k My Mother F**king Life	FMM
F**k No	FN
F**k Off	FO
F**k Off And Google	FOAG
F**k Yes	FY
F**k You	42
F**k You	43
F**k You	FU
F**king Bulls**t	FBS
F**king Google It	FGI
F**king Love My Life	FLML
F**king Love Sucks	FLS
F**king Magic	FM
F**king New Guy	FNG
F**king Super Sweet	FSS
F**king Sweet	FS
F**king Ugly	FUG
F**king With You	FWY

Fabulous	FAB
Face To Face	FTF
Face up deal (online gaming)	FUD
Facebook	FB
Facebook chat	FBC
Facebook friend	FBFR
Face-to-Face	F2F
Fair Market Value	FMV
Fake false or over embellished Tweets	BULLTWITT
Falling asleep at keyboard	FAAK
Falling off my chair	FOMC
Falling off my chair laughing	FOMCL
Family member's house	323
Fancy expensive CB radio	BIG RIG
Fan-F**king-Tastic	FFT
Fan-Tan-Stic	FTS
Faster Than A Speeding Bullet	FTASB
Faster Than Light	FTL
Fat boy food (pizza/burgers/fries)	FBF
Fat Chance	FC
Father-in-law	FIL
FCC	BIG CHARLIE
Fear Of Being Left Out	FOBLO
Fear of Failure	FOF
Fear Of Missing Out	FOMO
Fear/Uncertainty/Doubt	FUD
Feel Better	434
Feel unique for life	FUFL
Feelings of rage experienced as a result of a Twitter post	TWITTERAGE

Fell off chair laughing	FOCL
Female	BEAVER
Female	F
Female Cop	BEAVER BEAR
Female genitalia	TWAT
Female passenger	SEAT COVER
Feminine	FEM
Fiesta/Party	FSTA
Fill In The Blank	FITB
Fine	59
Fine	5N
Fine	F9
Fine by me	FBM
Fine with me	FWM
Fingers crossed	FC
First Come First Served	FCFS
First In - Still Here	FISH
First In First Out	FIFO
Fish/fishy	> ><<*>
Fitness Center	311
Flatbed trailer with ribs and soft top	CONESTOGA
Flatbed Truck With Sides And A Top Cover	COVERED WAGON
Florida	BIKINI STATE
Follow Friday (Twitter slang)	FF
Follow up	FU
For	4
For *freak'*sakes	FFS
For adults only	4AO
For better or worse	FBOW

For Crying Out Loud	4COL
For crying out loud	FC'INGO
For crying out loud	FCOL
For fun	4FN
For our eyes only	FOEO
For real though	FRT
For Sale	FS
For some reason	FSR
For The Loss	FTL
For The F**king Loss	FTFL
For The F**king Win	FTFW
For The Mother F**king Loss	FTMFL
For The Mother F**king Win	FTMFW
For The Win	FTW
For What It's Worth	FWIW
For you to see	4U2C
For Your Amusement	FYA
For Your Entertainment	FYE
For your eyes only	4YEO
For your eyes only	FYEO
For Your F**king Information	FYFI
For Your Information	FYI
Foreigner	4NR
Forever	4EVA
Forever	4EVR
Forever	4va
Forever	7
Forever and ever	4EAE
Forever in my heart	FIMH
Forget	4GET
Forget It - Cut And Run	FICAR
Forget it - I'm out of here	FIIOOH

Formerly known as	FKA
Forrest City Arkansas	BAR CITY
Forward	FW
Fouled Up Beyond All Recognition	FUBAR
Fouled Up Beyond All Repair	FUBAR
Fouled Up Beyond Belief	FUBB
Four Wheeler (standard van or auto)	4W
Frankly I couldn't care a less	FICCL
Freak Me Out	82
Freaking cracking up	FCU
Free for all (online gaming)	FFA
Free stuff and giveaways	SWAG
Free to play (online gaming)	F2P
Freightliner Truck	FREIGHT SHAKER
French kiss	:->*<-:
French kiss	FK
Frequently Asked Questions	FAQ
Frequently used English slang expletive	BLOODY
Friday	055
Friend of A Friend	FOAF
Friend with benefits	FWB
Friends are friends for ever	FAFFE
Friend's Place	309
From My Point Of View	FMPOV
From The Article	FTA
From the bottom of my heart	FTBOMH
From The F**king Article	FTFA
Frown	:(

F**k the world	FTW
Full card (online gaming)	FC
Full glass	\~/
Full Up Ready To Burst	FURTB
Fully Acknowledged	FACK
Funny as *freak*	FAF
Future husband	FH
G Descriptions	
Garbage In - Garbage Out	GIGO
Gay best friend	GBF
Gee	G
Gee I Don't Know	GIDK
Gee I Wish I'd Said That	GIWIST
General term for the Twitter Universe	TWITOSPHERE
Genius	G9
Gentle warning like "Hmm? What did you say?"	;S
Get a *freaking* clue	GAFC
Get a clue	GAC
Get A F**king Life	GAFL
Get A F**king Move On	GAFMO
Get A Life	GAL
Get a life	GTL
Get a life dude	GTLD
Get A Move On	GAMO
Get back to work	GBTW
Get In Line	69999
Get In Line	GIL
Get off my back	GOMB

Get Off Your Fat Ass	GOYFA
Get On With It	GOWI
Get out of here	GOOH
Get Out or Get Off	GO
Get over it	GOI
Get over it already	GOIA
Get right with God	GRWG
Get the *freak* out	GTFO
Get the *freak* outta here	GTFOH
Get the frick outtta my life	GTFOML
Get together with me	207
Gift in crib (online gaming)	GIC
Giggle	*G*
Giggle	G
Giggling my A$$ off	GMAO
Giggling my butt off	GMBO
Giggling out loud	GOL
Giggling to myself	GTM
Girl	GRL
Girl Friend	GF
Girlfriend	G/F
Girls' Night Out	GNO
Give it a rest	GIAR
Give it all you got	GIAYG
Give me	GIMME
Give Me A Break	GMAB
Give Me A F**king Break	GMFAB
Glad to see you	GTCU
Glad we had this little chat	GWHTLC
Glass (drink)	\ /
Go ahead	GA
Go F**king Google It	GFGI

Go fly a kite	GFAK
Go for a Beer?	24-24-24
Go for it	GFI
Go for it!	495
Go Google It	GGI
Go take a hike	GTAH
Go take a walk	GTAW
Go to	110
Go to	GO2
Go To F**king Google	GTFG
Go To F**king Hell	GTFH
Go To Google	GTG
Go to heck	GTH
Go To Hell	GTH
God bless	GB
God Bless America	GBA
God bless you	GBU
God F**king Damn It	GFDI
God F**king Damnit	GFD
God Save The King	GSTK
God Save The Queen	GSTQ
Going	GOIN
Going Faster	XLR8
Going for coffee	G4C
Going now	112
Going to	GONNA
Going to read mail	GTRM
Going to sleep	22222222
Gone for now	GFN
Good	GD
Good	GUD
Good - N' You?	GNU

Good afternoon	49
Good F**king Game	GFG
Good F**king Luck	GFL
Good F**king Story	GFS
Good Friend	6771
Good game - you too	GGU2
Good Game (online gaming)	GG
Good game all (online gaming)	GGA
Good game everyone (online gaming)	GGE1
Good hand (online gaming)	GH
Good job	GJ
Good job partner	GJP
Good Luck	GL
Good luck - have fun (online gaming)	GL/HF
Good luck all (online gaming)	GLA
Good Luck and Good Hunting	GLGH
Good luck everyone (online gaming)	GLE
Good luck everyone (online gaming)	GLE1
Good luck next game (online gaming)	GLNG
Good luck to you (online gaming)	GL2U
Good morning	47
Good morning	99
Good Morning	GM
Good night	45
Good Night	GDNI8
Good night	GN

Good night	GN8
Good night	GNIGHT
good night	G'NIGHT
Good night	GNITE
Good night - Sweet dreams	45-56
Good night - Sweet dreams	GNSD
Good night all	GNA
Good night everyone	GNE1
Good night sleep tight don't let the bed bugs bite	GNSTDLTBBB
Good One	G1
Good shot	GS
Good split (online gaming)	GS
Good Story	GS
Good to go	GTG
Good to see you	G2CU
Good try	GT
Goodbye	**poof**
Goodbye	GB
Goodbye	POOF
Good-bye (Italian)	CIAO
Good-bye (signoff)	ABTA
Goodnight	45
Google It	GI
Gorgeous	GRGZ
Got a second?	GAS
Got my vote	GMV
Got tagged for a speeding ticket	BIT ON THE BRITCHES
Got to	GOSTA
Got to Go	G2G
Got To Go	GTG

Got to go eat my breakfast	GTGEMB
Got to go eat my dinner	GTGEMD
Got to go eat my lunch	GTGEML
Got to go I'll see you later	G2GICYAL8ER
Got to go to sleep	GTGTS
Got to run	G2R
Got to tell u (you)	G2TU
Got weed?	420
Got you	GOTCHA
Got your message	214
Gotta get me some of that	GGMSOT
Gotta Get Outa Here	GGOH
Gotta Go	GG
Gotta go now	GGN
Gotta Go Pee	GGP
Gracias/Thanks	ASIAS
Gratuitous picture of yourself	GPOY
Great	GR8
Great (or good) to see you	GTSY
Great for life	GR8FL
Great Minds Think Alike	GMTA
Greetings and salutations	GAS
Grim File Reaper	GFR
Grin	<G>
Grin	G
Grin - Duck and Weave	GDW
Grinning - Ducking and Running	GD&R
Grinning - ducking and running	GDR
Grinning - Ducking and Running Fast	GD&RF
Grinning - Ducking and Walking	GD&WVF

Very Fast	
Grinning - ducking/running	GD/R
Grinning Running and Ducking	GR&D
Grow up	93
Guffawing loudly waking up the neighborhood	GLWTN
Guy in real life	GIRL

H Descriptions

Ha Ha	8484
Ha ha ha very funny	HHHVF
Ha Ha Only Joking	HHOJ
Ha Ha Only Kidding	HHOK
Hacks	HAX
Half Life (online gaming)	HL
Hang On A Second	HOAS
Hang up the phone	203
Hanging Head In Shame	HHIS
Hanging On Your Every Word	HOYEW
Happy Birthday	121212
Happy Birthday	58
Happy Birthday	H-BDAY
Happy Birthday/Anniversary	601
Happy Father's Day	H-FDAY
Happy Holidays to You and Yours	HHTYAY
Happy Mother's Day	H-MDAY
Happy New Year	HNY
Happy New Year	HNY
Hard to hear	H2H
Hard to recognize dude	HTRD

Hashtag/Pound Sign/Number Sign used in Twitter to make it easier to find messages with a specific theme	#
Hate	H8
Hate to be you	H8TTU
Hauling A Very Light OR Empty Trailer	DISPATCHER BRAINS
Have	HV
Have a good night	HAGN
Have a good one	HAG1
Have a good one	HAGO
Have a great day	HADG
Have A Great Day	HAGD
Have a great summer	HAGS
Have A Nice Day	HAND
Have a nice day	HND
Have a safe trip	KEEP SHINY SIDE UP/THE RUBBER SIDE DOWN
Have a wonderful day	HAWT
Have fun	HF
Have to	HAFTA
Have to	HAV2
Have to eat	H2E
Head	HED
Head up butt head	HUBH
Head up your *butt*	HUYA
Heart	<3
Heart or love (more 3s indicate bigger heart)	<33

Heavy Metal Music	\M/
Helicopter Parents	HP
Hello	07734
Hello	HALOOO
Hello (Spanish)	HOLA
Hello again	RE
Hello everyone	HED
Hells Angels (H=8th letter; A=1st letter of alphabet)	81
Help	111
Help	SOS
Here	AKI
Heroic Violent Hold (online gaming)	HVH
Hey	A
Hey	YO
Hey sexy	HSX
Hi	14
Hi	5
Hi again	REHI
Hi Cutie / handsome	385
Hi There	HT
Hi*	14
High five	^5
Highway Patrol	FULL GROWN BEAR
Hit points / Health points (online gaming)	HP
Hitting Bottom And Starting To Dig	HBASTD
Hoe	304
Hoes be Hoes	HBH

Hola/Hello (Spanish)	HLA
Hold on	H/O
Holy Cow	HC
Holy F**king S**t	HFS
Holy flipping animal crackers	HFAC
Holy S**t	HS
Home	312
Home Work	HM
Homework	HMWRK
Homework	HW
Hope That Helps!	HTH
Hope to see you soon	H2CUS
Hope you're feeling better	603
Hope you're feeling better	98-6
Hospital	313
Hot For You	H4U
Hotmail Instant Messenger	HIM
House of worship	304
Houston Texas	ASTRODOME CITY
Houston TX	THE DOME CITY
How about a kiss	HAAK
How about you?	HAU
How are you?	HRU
How 'bout you?	HBU
How Do You Like Them Apples?	HDYLTA
How far away are you	QRB
How is traffic	QAI
How Should I Know	HSIK
How you doing?	HUD

How You Feel Really?	HYFR
Hug	46
Hug	H
Hug back	HB
Hugs	59173
Hugs & kisses	406
Hugs & kisses	H&K
Hugs & Kisses	XOXO
Hugs (as in hugs and kisses XOXO)	O
Hugs and kisses	(( )):**
Hugs and Kisses	080808
Hugs and Kisses	25252525
Hugs and Kisses	406
Hugs and Kisses	436
Hugs and kisses	88
Hugs And Kisses	HAK
Huh?	?
Hurry back soon	HBS
Hurry up	52
Hurry up	HU
Husband	HUS
Husband over shoulder	HOS

I Descriptions

I (I've) got nothing	IGN
I already ate	IA8
I am a doctor	IAAD
I am a lawyer	IAAL
I am an accountant	IAAA
I am not a crook	IANAC

I Am Not A Lawyer (but)	IANAL
I Am Not A Lawyer but ….	IANALB
I am out (of here)	IAO
I am so bored	IMSB
I am sorry	IMS
I am the man	IMTM
I ate	1-8
I ate	1-8
I Beg To Differ	IBTD
I beg your pardon	IBYP
I believe you	IBU
I can't even discuss it	ICEDI
I can't meet you	202
I can't wait	ICW
I could fall in love with you	ICFILWU
I couldn't agree more	ICAM
I dare you	IDY
I don't believe it	IDBI
I Don't Care	IDC
I Don't F**king Care	IDFC
I Don't F**king Give A S**t	IDFGAS
I Don't F**king Know	IDFK
I don't get it	IDGI
I don't give a *freak*	IDGAF
I don't give a darn	IDGAD
I Don't Give A S**t	IDGAS
I don't know	404
I Don't Know	IDK
I don't know	IDNO
I don't know	IDUNNO
I Don't Know Tell Me What It Means	IDKTMWIM

I don't love you	1443
I don't really care	IDRC
I don't really know	IDRK
I Don't Remember	IDR
I don't think	IDT
I don't think so	IDTS
I don't understand what you mean	?
I don't wanna talk to you	IDWTTU
I don't want to talk about it	IDW2TAI
I F**king Hate My Life	IFHML
I F**king Hate You	IFHU
I F**king Love You	IFLU
I F**king Love You	IFLY
I feel sick	5900
I feel your pain	IFYP
I forever love you	IFLY
I Give a F**K	IGAF
I got high tonight	IGHT
I got this	IGT
I got to (go) pee	IGP
I got to go	IGTG
I got to run	IG2R
I Hate My Life	IHML
I Hate This F**king Place	IHTFP
I Hate This Place	IHTP
I hate you	182
I Hate You	4040
I Hate You	IHU
I Hate You So F**king Much	IHUSFM
I Hate You So Much	IHUSM
I have a comment	!

I have a question	?
I have a question for you	?4U
I have finished talking	BACK OUT
I Have No Clue	IHNC
I Have No F**king Clue	IHNFC
I have no idea	IHNI
I have to go	IH2G
I hear u	IHU
I just farted	IJF
I Just Want To Know	IJWTK
I Just Want To Say	IJWTS
I knew it	IKI
I know	IK
I know	INO
I know right?	IKR
I know that	IKT
I Know What You Mean	IKWUM
I Know What's Right	IKWR
I Know What's Wrong	IKWW
I know you	IKU
I Know You Are But What Am I?	IKYABWAI
I Like You	341
I like you	ILQ
I Love My F**king Life	ILMFL
I Love My Life	ILML
I Love You	143
I love you	143
I love you	i<3u
I Love You	ILU
I Love You	ILY
I love you (8 letters - 3 words -	831

1 meaning)	
I love you (ILY is 459 on phone keypad)	459
I love you (Italian)	TI-AMO
I love you back	360
I love you harder	ILYH
I love you man	ILUM
I love you more	ILUM
I Love You So F**king Much	ILUSFM
I love you so freaking much	ILUSFM
I love you so much	1432222222
I Love You So Much	ILUSM
I love you so much	ILYSM
I love you too	1432
I love you too	ILY2
I Might Add	IMA
I miss u (you)	IMU
I miss you	10000001
I Miss You	123
I miss you	607
I Miss You So F**king Much	IMYSFM
I Miss You So Much	IMYSM
I Need A Favor	074
I Need Information	411
I need some information	411
I need to hold you forever	IN2HYF
I need to talk to you alone	121
I Only Have Eyes For You	IOHE4U
I owe you	IOU
I really don't care	IRDC
I really don't know	IRDK
I rest my case	IRMC

I See	IC
I See What You Mean	ISWYM
I Still Love You	1543
I still love you	ISLY
I think I know that	ITIKT
I think not	ITN
I thought you knew	ITYK
I Thought You Knew That	ITYKT
I too (me too)	I2
I want a way out	IWAWO
I want Love	444
I Want To Ask A Question	IWTAAQ
I want you	1-0351123-400
I want you	122
I Will Always Love You	IWALU
I will key you later	IWKYL
I wish you were here	IWUWH
I wonder	1DR
I'm So Sure	ISS
I'm So Sure You Get The Idea!	ISSYGTI
Idiot Behind Keyboard	IBK
Idiot wrapped in a moron	IWIAM
If I Recall Correctly...	IIRC
If I Remember Correctly	IIRC
If I Were You	IIWY
If It Ain't Broke DON'T Fix It	IIABDFI
If It Were Me	IIWM
If The Shoe Fits Wear It	ITSFWI
If you know what I mean	IUKWIM
If you know what I mean	IYKWIM
If you say so	IUSS
If You Say So	IYSS

If You See What I Mean	IYSWIM
I'll	ILL
I'll be late	ILBL8
I'll get you	212
I'm almost completely (99 & 44/100%) bored	99-44-100
I'm back	IB
I'm blowing you a kiss	365
I'm bored	125
I'm busy	183
I'm Confused	0121
I'm dreaming of you	124
I'm feeling kinda wicked	90210
I'm feeling mighty alone right now	0001000
I'm feeling mighty alone/left out right now!	0001000
I'm free	1-800
I'm gonna get even with you	8642
I'm having a bad day	13
I'm having a bad day and it's getting old	13-30
I'm heading to the beach	024
I'm here	92134-1111
I'm Home	24
I'm in trouble	119
I'm Into You	IMN2U
I'm mad	66
I'm mad at you	609
I'm not a lawyer	INAL
I'm not going to Beep you again	618
I'm on my way	54321

I'm out of gas	710
I'm out of gas (Read upside down)	710
I'm Outta Here	IOH
I'm pissed off	197
I'm ready to explode	54321
I'm sad	70
I'm scared	610
I'm so angry	<GRRR>
I'm so tired I think I'm Gonna die	STTGD
I'm sorry	611
I'm sorry for you-know-what	350
I'm thinking about you	612
I'm Tired	010
I'm with you	141
I'm with you thru thick & thin	470
Important CB'er	ACE
In	N
In a Manner of Speaking	IAMOS
In a traffic jam	216
In Accordance With	IAW
In Any Case	IAC
In Any Event	IAE
In Before Dark	IBD
In Before the Lock	IBTL
In case you missed it (Twitter slang)	ICYMI
In F**king Control	IFC
In Jail	IJ
In My Absolutely Honest Opinion	IMAHO

In My Arrogant Opinion	IMAO
In My Biased Opinion	IMBO
In My Considered Opinion	IMCO
In My Experience	IME
In My F**king Opinion	IMFO
In My Humble Opinion	IMHO
In My Not So Humble Opinion	IMNSHO
In My Opinion	IMO
In My Point Of View	IMPOV
In No Particular Order	INPO
In Other Words	IOW
In over my head	IOMH
In Real Life	IRL
In reference to	118
In Regard To	RE
In Regards To	IRT
In route	209
In The Final Analysis	ITFA
In The Real World	ITRW
In this thread	ITT
In your opinion	IYO
Incoming (online gaming)	INC
Indianapolis IN	INDY 500
Indifferent	:-i
Insert Your Favorite Ethnic Group	IYFEG
Instant Messager	IM
Intel inside/idiot outside	IIIO
Interference from a station on another channel	BLEEDING/BL EEDOVER
Internet	INET
Internet Service Provider	ISP

Interstate	BIG ROAD
Invite	INV
Is everything OK?	10-4
It could be worse	ICBW
It doesn't matter to me; what do you want to do?	50-50
It Would Be Nice If	IWBNI
Item is completed	205
Item is not completed	206
It's okay	S'OK
It's late - Get home!	613
It's Over	1023
It's possible; there's a chance	10-2-1
It's quitting time	9-5
It's The Accounting Man (financial blogs)	ITAM
I've got a secret	007
I've got a secret	405
I've got an easy question	101
I've got something stupid to tell you	099
I've taken care of it	213

J Descriptions

Jackpot (online gaming)	JP
Je le savais/I knew it	JE LE SAV
Jealous	JELLY
Jesus loves you	JLU
Joint venture	JV
Joking	J/K
Jumping with joy	JWJ

Just A Minute	JAM
Just a second	JA2ND
Just A Second	JAS
Just Another Animal	JAA
Just Another F**king Animal	JAFA
Just Another F**king Observer	JAFO
Just Another Observer	JAO
Just asking	J/A
Just checking	JC
Just Chilling	JC
Just Do It	JDI
Just F**king Do It	JFDI
Just F**king Google It	JFGI
Just F**king With You	JFWY
Just For Fun	J4F
Just For Fun	JFF
Just for giggles	J4G
Just For Information	JFI
Just for your information	JFYI
Just Google It	JGI
Just In Case	JIC
Just joking	JJ
Just joking around	JJA
Just kidding	07
Just Kidding	46
Just Kidding	JK
Just let me know	JLMK
Just like that	JLT
Just messing	JM
Just My Humble Opinion	JMHO
Just My Opinion	JMO
Just playing	J/P

Just playing	JP
Just say it	JSI
Just stop talking	JST
Just teasing	JT
Just thinking of you	020202
Just to let you know	J2LUK
Just to let you know	JTLUK
Just to let you know	JTLYK
Just wanted to say Hi	614
Just wondering	J/W
Just wondering	JW
Just Wondering	JWK

K Descriptions

Kansas City KS	Bright Lights
Karma(what goes around comes around)	404
Keep In Touch	KIT
Keep It Simple Stupid	KISS
Keep it Sweetly Simple	KISS
Keep Parents Clueless	KPC
Keep up the good work	KUTGW
Keep Your Fingers Crossed	KYFC
Key me (when you get in)	KEYME
Keyboard	K/B
Keyboard	KB
keys	419
Kick butt (online gaming)	KB
Kid over shoulder	KOS
Kill then steal (online gaming)	KS
Killed In Action	KIA

Kiss	:-)*(-:
Kiss	X
Kiss (mimics the sound made when kissing through the air)	MWAH
Kiss for you	KFY
Kiss me	KM
Kiss my *a*	KMA
Kiss My F**king A$$	KMFA
Kiss My Italian Ass	KMIA
Kiss my keister	KMK
Kiss my tushie	KMT
Kiss on cheek	KOC
Kiss on lips	KOL
Kiss on the cheek	KOTC
Kiss On The Lips	KOTL
Knock on wood	KOW
Knocked Up (pregnant)	KN
Know How You Feel	KHYF
Know it all	KIA
Know what I mean?	KNIM
Know What I Mean?	KWIM
Knowledge	KNOW
Knowledge	NOWL
Knowledge In - Bullshit Out	KIBO
Knoxville TN	K-Town
L Descriptions	
Language - Sex and violence	LSV
Laptop of death	LTOD
Last In First Out	LIFO
Late	L8

Late (meant to be read upside down)	87
Later	L8R
Later	LT8R
Later	LTR
Later dude	LD
Later gator	L8RG8R
Laugh	L
Laugh a little	LAL
Laugh in my tummy	LIMT
Laugh My Butt Off	LMBO
Laughing	XD
Laughing (In Thai language '5' is pronounced 'ha')	55555
Laughing (Wide Open Smiley Mouth)	XO
Laughing back at you	LBAY
Laughing but not out loud	LBNOL
Laughing but serious	LBS
Laughing but very serious	LBVS
Laughing head off	LHO
Laughing My A$$ Off	LMAO
Laughing My F**king A$$ Off	LMFAO
Laughing my fat a** off	LMFAO
Laughing my freaking *a* off	LMFAO
Laughing My Head Off	LMHO
Laughing my socks off	LMSO
Laughing non stop	LNS
Laughing on the inside	LOTI
Laughing Out F**king Loud	LOFL
Laughing Out Loud	LOL
Laughing out loud hysterically	LOLH

Laughing Quietly To Myself	LQTM
Laughing Quite Loudly	LQL
Laughing So F**king Hard	LSFH
Laughing So Hard	LSH
Laughing So Hard My Belly Hurts	LSHMBH
Laughing To Myself	LTM
Laughing to self	L2S
Laughing to Self	LTS
Laughing to Yourself	LTY
Laughing Too Hard To Type	LTHTT
Laughing without smiling	LWOS
Laughs Out Loud	707
Learn to play	L2P
Leave Me Alone	LMA
Leave my name out	LMNK
Leaving easy reach of keyboard	LERK
Left for day	LFD
Left Lane [Fast Lane]	HAMMER LANE
Left voice mail	LVM
Let me know	LEMENO
Let Me Know	LMK
Let Me See	LMS
Let's Just Be Friends	LJBF
Let's cruise	55
Let's fly	747
Let's get high	420
Let's get high	LGH
Lets get together	69
Let's go out	1925

Let's go sailing	1492
Let's go to Hawaii	5-0
Let's have a drink	21
Let's have sex	LH6
Let's have sex	LHSX
Lets hit the road	66
Let's meet in real life	LMIRL
Let's rock on	LRO
Lets you stay connected through short messages called 'tweets'	TWITTER
Life is good	LIG
Life is short	LIS
Life's A Bitch - Then You Die	LABATYD
Like	LYK
Like duh! Obviously!	LDO
Like I care	LIC
Like my status (Facebook)	LMS
Like to come	L2K
Like to go?	L2G
Linear Amp	AFTER BURNER
LinkedIn	LI
Lips are sealed	:-#
Liquor	LIK
List of acronyms	LOA
Listening to music	d-_-b
Little	LIL
Live long and prosper	1701
Live Long And Prosper	LLAP
Livin it up	LIU
Living the dream	LTD

Location	20
Long Day	LD
Long distance	LD
Long F**king Day	LFD
Long Time No See	LTNS
Long Time No Type	LTNT
Looking for group (online gaming)	LFG
Looking for more (online gaming)	LFM
Loose Straps Mean Floppy T*ts	LSMFT
Lord help me	LHM
Lord help us	LHU
Lord of The Rings (online gaming)	LOTR
Los Angeles CA	SHAKY-TOWN
Loser beyond repair	LBR
Lost	113
Lost in translation	LNT
Lots and Lots of Thunderous Applause	LLTA
Lots of Love	LOL
Lots of love	LOLOV
Lot's Of Love	LOLV
Lots Of Luck	LOL
Loud mouth - or Someone who uses a lot of profanity	BUCKET MOUTH
Louisville KY	DERBY CITY
Love - Later God bless	LLGB
Love me	LM
Love My Life	LML
Love Of My Life	LOML

Love Sucks	LS
Love to go	L2G
Love ya	LY
Love you	<3u
Love You	LY
Love You Like A Brother	LYLAB
Love You Like A Sister	LYLAS
Love you like crazy	LYLC
Love you long time	LULT
Love you lots	LYL
Love You Miss You	LYMY
Love You So F**king Much	LYSFM
Love You So Much	LYSM
Love You With All My Heart	LUWAMH

M Descriptions

Mack Truck	BIG MACK
Mack Truck	BULLDOG
Mad for it	MFI
Made with love by	MWLB
Make a decision	MAD
Male	M
Male or Female	MOF
Male or female?	MORF
Mamma's boy	MB
Mamma's boy	MOMBOY
Mana points (online gaming)	MP
Management	MGMT
Manuscript	MS
Margaritas dude! (Cinco de Mayo)	05-05

Marijuana	420
Marijuana	ACE
Mark my words	MMW
Mary Jane (Marijuana)	MJ
Massively Multiplayer Online	MMO
Massively Multiplayer Online Role-Playing Games	MMORPG
Mate	M8
Matter Of Fact	MOF
Matter Of Opinion	MOO
May God bless	MGB
May the force be with you	MTFBWU
Maybe	11
Maybe	5050
Maybe	50-50
Me Too	1250
Meet	114
Meet in real life	MIRL
Meeting	MTG
Meeting Group	306
Meeting or Appointment	316
Member Of Same Sex	MOSS
Member Of The Appropriate Sex	MOTAS
Member Of The Opposite Sex	MOOS
Member Of The Opposite Sex	MOTOS
Member Of The Same Sex	MOTSS
Memphis TN	BIG M
Mensaje/Message (Spanish)	MNSG
Merry Christmas	1225
Merry Christmas	12-25
Merry Christmas	MC

Mesmerizing (online gaming)	MEZ
Message	MSG
Message Me Back	MMB
Message of the day	MOTD
Microsoft	M$
Mile Marker	YARD STICK
Milwaukee WI	BEER CITY
Milwaukee WI	BEER TOWN
Mind your own (business)	MYO
Mind your own business	460
Mind Your Own Business	MYOB
Mind your own darn business	MYODB
Mind Your Own F**king Business	MYOFB
Minute	MIN
Miss Me?	193
Miss U (you)	MU
Miss you so	MYS
Miss you so much	MUSM
Missing In Action	MIA
Missing you a lot	MUAL
Mission Impossible	MIM
Mission Improbable	MIM
Mistell (mistaken chat message - please disregard)	MT
Mixed up	:~/
Mmm - Okay	MKAY
Mobile	MOB
Moderator	MOD
Modified Retweet	MRT
Mom behind shoulder	MBS
Mom Over Shoulder	MOS

Monday	011
Money	BEAVER BAIT
Money growth info systems	MGIS
More later	ML8TR
More to follow	M2F
More to follow	MTF
Mother F**king Bitch	MFB
Mother F**king Mother F**ker	MFMF
Motorcycle	CROTCH ROCKET
Motorcycle Cop	Evil Kenevil
Mouth open in surprise	:-O
Move Faster	HAMMER DOWN
Moving Right Along	MRA
Mug of hot coffee or tea	@[ ]~~
Multiple Letter Acronym	MLA
Multiple unsuccessful attempts (at/to) humor	MUAAH
Multi-tasker	MTTSKR
Multitasking	MTTSKG
Music Store	329
Music video	MV
Must be nice	MBN
My (or your) two cents worth	0.02
My bad	M/B
My Boss Is Listening	MBIL
My Dad is a cop	MDIAC
My dad's calling	MDC
My Eyes Glaze Over	MEGO
My friend calls	MFC
My heart belongs to you	MHB2U

My Honest Opinion	MHO
My mom's calling	MMC
My own opinion	MOO
My Sexy Baby	244
My Sexy Baby	280

N Descriptions

Naked in front of computer	NIFOC
Nashville TN	GUITAR CITY
Near a phone	200
Need for Speed (online gaming)	NFS
Need you	27
Negative /No	116
Network	NW
Never	937
Never	NVR
Never Again Volunteer Yourself	NAVY
Never F**king Mind	NVRFM
Never Heard Of Him/Her	NHOH
Never heard of that	NHOT
Never mind	54
Never Mind	NM
Never Mind	NVM
Never Mind	NVRM
New Guy	NG
New person with limited skills	NEWBIE
New With Out Tags	NWOT
New With Tags	NWT
New York NY	BIG APPLE
Newbie	N00B

Newly qualified teacher	NQT
Nice crib (online gaming)	NC
Nice doing business with you	NDBWY
Nice double (online gaming)	ND
Nice hand (online gaming)	NH
Nice meld (online gaming)	NM
Nice one	N1
Nice one	NCE1
Nice roll (online gaming)	NR
Nice score (online gaming)	NS
Nice split (online gaming)	NS
Nice to know	N2N
Nice to meet you	NTMU
Nice to see you	NTCU
Nice try	NT
Nickname (Userid or CB nickname)	HANDLE
Night	9T
Night	N8
Night	NYT
Night Club	307
Nightclub/Singles bar	BEAVER PALACE
Nighty-night	99
No	17
No Problem	NP
No *freaking* way	NFW
No answer	210
No Big Deal	NBD
No boyfriend since birth	NBSB
No Clue	NC
No Comment	N/C

No Comment	NC
No Doubt	ND
No F**king Clue	NFC
No F**king Doubt	NFD
No F**king Good	NFG
No F**king Problem	NFP
No girlfriend since birth	NGSB
No Good	NG
No guts - No glory	NGNG
No I meant u	NIMU
No I meant you	NIMY
No idea	NI
No joke?	~~!!~~
No kidding	NK
No later than	NLT
No need to reply	NNTR
No one	NO1
No Pasa Nada/Nothing's happening (Spanish)	NPN
No permanent address	NPA
No Questions Asked	NQA
No reply necessary	NRN
No Response Necessary	NRN
No spam!!	[X]
No strings attached	NSA
No Such Thing As A Free Lunch	NSTAAFL
No Thank You	NTU
No Thank You	NTY
No Thanks Needed	NTN
No way	N/W
No way	NW

No way out	NWO
No! No! No!	90*90*90
Non technical person who just knows how to turn the rig on	APPLIANCE OPERATOR
None for me	NFM
None Of Your Business	NOYB
None Of Your F**king Business	NOYFB
Non-playing character (online gaming)	NPC
North American Free Trade Agreement	NAFTA
Nose laugh	NL
Not A Clue	NAC
Not a darn thing	NADT
Not A F**king Clue	NAFC
Not a lot of people know that	NALOPKT
Not an emergency - but very important!	811
Not Applicable	NA
Not available	120
Not Available	NA
Not bad for a beginner (online gaming)	NBFAB
Not even close	NEC
Not for me	NFM
Not for sale	NFS
Not for work	NFW
Not going to wait any longer	218
Not gonna happen	NGH
Not gonna lie	NGL
Not in My Back Yard	NIMBY
Not in reach of keyboard	NIROK

Not In The F**king Mood	NITFM
Not In The Mood	NITM
Not Invented Here	NIH
Not much	N/M
Not Much	NM
Not much - You?	NMU
Not much here	NMH
Not My F**king Problem	NMFP
Not my number	NMN
Not My Opinion	NMO
Not My Problem	NMP
Not On My Watch	NOMW
Not possible	NTPBL
Not safe for work	NSFW
Not safe for work	NSFW
Not Safe For Workplace Viewing	NSFW
Not sure if spelled right	NSISR
Not that easy	NTE
Not That It Matters	NTIM
Not That It Matters Much	NTIMM
Not To Worry	NTW
Not too much	N2M
Not yet	N/Y
Not yet	NY
Not Your Business	NYB
Note to self	NTS
Nothing In - Nothing Out	NINO
Nothing much	NM
Nothing much just chilling	NMJC
Nothing too much	N2M
Nothing ventured - Nothing	NVNG

gained	
Now I get it	NIGI
Now or never	NON
Now That You Mention It	NTYMI
Now Used As A Term For A Homosexual	GOOD BUDDY
Now we dance	2-2
Now we dance; shall we dance?	2-2
Number of items needed for win (online gaming)	1TG
Number of items needed for win (online gaming)	2TG

O Descriptions

Obligatory	OB
Obligatory On-Topic Comment	OOTC
Obviously	OBV
Of course	OFC
Off The Top Of My Head	OTTOMH
Off to bed	OTB
Off to work	OTW
Off topic (discussion forums)	OT
Oh - I'm back	OIB
Oh - Ok cool	OKC
Oh baby	OB
Oh boy	OB
Oh brother	OB
Oh By The Way	OBTW
Oh F**king Well	OFW
Oh God it's Monday	OGIM

Oh I know you will	OINYW
Oh I See	OIC
Oh Mother God	OMG
Oh my	OM
Oh my *freaking* God	OMFG
Oh my aching *A*	OMAA
Oh my aching butt	OMAB
Oh My F**king Word	OMFW
Oh My God	OMG
Oh My God (World of Warcraft)	ZOMG
Oh my God you got to be kidding	OMGYG2BK
Oh my gosh	OMG
Oh my gosh you suck	OMGYS
Oh My Word	OMW
Oh No Not Again	ONNA
Oh No Not This Again	ONNTA
Oh No You Didn't	ONYD
Oh okay	OOK
Oh really?	ORLY
Oh Well	OW
Oh What the heck	OWTH
Ohio	BUCKEYE STATE
OK	K
OK - Just Stop Talking	KJST
Okay! Okay!	KK
Old lady	OL
Old man	OM
On a Totally Unrelated Subject	OATUS
On An Unrelated Subject	OAUS
On my way	OMW

On phone	OP
On Second Thought	OST
On the Floor (laughing)	OTF
On the hunt for a women	BEAVER PATROL
On the Other Hand	OTOH
On The Other Other Hand	OTOOH
On the phone	OTP
On The Third Hand	OTTH
On your own	OYO
Once	1CE
One for all and all for one	14AA41
One in a million	1NAM
One of a Kind	OOAK
One of these days	OOTD
One who subscribes to receives your updates on Twitter	FOLLOWER
One-to-one (private chat initiation)	121
Online	OL
Online	ONL
Online auctions	OA
Online love	OLL
Only for you	O4U
Only joking	OJ
Onr of the many substitutes for F**KING	FLIPPIN
Operating system	OS
Operator indisposed	OI
Opponent (online gaming)	O
Or Best Offer	OBO
Or Words To That Effect	OWTTE

Orange Juice	OJ
Original gangster	OG
Original Poster (the one who started this discussion thread)	OP
Out of body	OOB
Out of character	OOC
Out of here	OOH
Out of mind	OOM
Out of place	OP
Out of the office	OOTO
Out To Lunch	OTL
Over	86
Over	OVA
Over (indicates the end of a communication)	O
Over and Out (used in Chats and IM to signal end of communication)	OO
Over Heard	OH
Over my dead body	OMDB
Over The Top	OTT
Over Time	OT
P Descriptions	
Packing a Big Gun	PABG
Page/text me now	883
Paid time off	PTO
Pain In (the) A$$	PIA
Pain in the *butt*	PITA
Pain In The A$$	PITA
Paper	PPR

Pardon Me For Barging In	PMFBI
Pardon Me For Breaking In	PMFBI
Pardon Me For Butting In	PMFBI
Pardon me for interrupting	PMFI
Pardon Me For Jumping In	PMFJI
Pardon My Barging In	PMBI
Pardon My Breaking In	PMBI
Pardon My Butting In	PMBI
Pardon My French	PMF
Pardon my interrupting	PMFI
Pardon My Jumping In	PMJI
Parent Alert Change Subject	P911
Parent is watching	9
Parent looking over shoulder	PLOS
Parent standing over shoulder	PSOS
Parent Teacher Organization	PTO
Parent to parent	P2P
Parents are coming	PAC
Parents are listening	PRL
Parents are watching	PAW
Parents coming into room alert	P911
Parents in room	PIR
Parents over heard	POH
Parents Over Shoulder (Sender is under scrutiny)	POS
Park	301
Partner (online gaming)	P
Party	BEER BUST
Party	PRTY
Pass the *freak* out	PTFO
Passed With Great Speed	BLEW MY DOORS OFF

Passing lane	BUMPER LANE
Patrol (online gaming)	PAT
Pawn	PWN
Pay to play (online gaming)	P2P
Peace	PZ
Peck on my cheek	POMC
Pee myself laughing	PMSL
Peeing in pants (laughing hard)	PIP
Peeing My Pants	PMP
Peer to peer	P2P
Pending pick-up	PPU
People	PEEPS
People	PPL
People Can't Memorize Computer Industry Acronyms	PCMCIA
People like us	PLU
People/parents are watching	PRW
Person Of Opposite Sex Sharing Living Quarters	POOSSLQ
Personal display (of) affection	PDA
Personal time off	PTO
Phone	FONE
Phonebook (e-mail)	PBOOK
Pick me up after school	222
Pick me up after school	222
Pick up group (online gaming)	PUG
Pick up kids	PUKS
Picture	PIC
Picture or it didn't happen	POIDH
Piece Of Crap	POC
Piece of S**t	POS

Pierdete/Get lost (Spanish)	PDT
Pill head	BEAN BOPPER
Pill Popper	BEAN POPPER
Pirated (illegally acquired) software	WAREZ
Piss and Moan	PNM
Piss on everything tomorrow is Saturday	POETS
Pizza	PZA
Plans changed	010
Plate	PL8
Played	PLD
Player character (online gaming)	PC
Player Kill	PK
Player versus player (online gaming)	PVP
PlayStation Portable	PSP
Please	001
Please	PLS
Please	PLZ
Please be careful out there!	395
Please call me	PCM
Please do not disturb	PDND
Please don't shoot	PDS
Please Don't Shout!(for those using All Caps)	PDS
Please explain that	PXT
Please Forgive Me	PFM
Please let me know	PLMK

Please reply	321
Please Retweet	PRT
Please send tell (online gaming)	PST
Please talk to me - I am bored	PTTMIAB
Please tell me	PLZTLME
Please Tell Me More	PTMM
Please! No Cursing Allowed Here	PNCAH
Poco/A little (Spanish)	PCO
Podcasting	PCT
Point of view	POV
Pokemon (online gaming)	PKMN
Police car located within a construction zone	CARE BEAR
Police car with a radar detector	BIG DOG
Police car with flashing lights on top	BUBBLE GUM MACHINE
Police In Helicopter	BEAR IN THE AIR
Police Officer	BEAR
Police Out Of Sight Hitting You With Radar	SHOOTING YOU IN THE BACK
Police Station	BEAR CAVE
Police station or jail	BEAR CAGE
Police Using Radar	TAKING PICTURES
Police with radar	BEAR TAKING PICTURES
Popcorn	****
Pornography	PORN
Posts published by micro	MICROPOST

bloggers	
Potion (online gaming)	POT
Praise the Lord	PTL
Pre Menstrual Syndrome	PMS
Precious	PRESH
President of the United States	POTUS
Press Lots Of Keys To Abort	PLOKTA
Pretty *freaking* tight	PFT
Pretty damn happy	PDH
Pretty Damn Quick	PDQ
Pretty darn happy	PDH
Pretty F**king Good	PFG
Pretty Good	PG
Pretty Hot	PH
Pretty Hot And Tempting	PHAT
Pretty young thing	PYT
Pretzels	&&&&
Primed (Lists all prime numbers under 10)	2357
Private joke	PJ
Private Message	PM
Private Message me	PMM
Privately owned vehicle (not a gov't vehicle)	POV
Probably	PRB
Probably	PROBLY
Probably	PROBS
Probably	PROLLY
Problem	PROB
Problem Encountered Between Chair And Keyboard (describes an inept operator)	PEBCAK

Prove It	1001
Public Domain	PD
Pure F**king Magic	PFM
Pure Freaking Magic	PMF
Pure Magic	PM
Pussy (Persian/Farsi similar to F**k)	KOS
Put in some sugar	PISS
Put Mind In Gear BEFORE Opening Mouth	PMIGBOM
Put on a happy face	POAHF
Put that in your pipe and smoke it	PTIYPASI

Q Descriptions

Quality control	QC
Question	QUES
Question for everyone	QFE
Queue	Q
Quick	QIK
Quick question	QQ
Quick/Simple/Easily Done	QSED
Quit F**king Talking	QTF
Quit laughing	QL
Quit Talking	QT
Quote of the day	QOTD
Quoted for idiocy	QFI
Quoted for irony	QFI
Quoted for Mother F**king Truth	QFMFT
Quoted For Truth	QFT

R Descriptions

Radar Detector	BIRD DOG
Radar trap ahead	BRUSH YOUR TEETH AND COMB YOUR HAIR
Radio At A Fixed Location	BASE STATION
Radio control signals	BE BOP
Rank Has Its Privileges	RHIP
Rate	R8
Read And Enjoyed But No Comment	RAEBNC
Read my lips baby	RMLB
Read my mail man	RMMM
Read the Article	RTA
Read The Manual	RTM
Read the *freaking* manual	RTFM
Read The Bloody Manual	RTBM
Read The Description	RTD
Read The F------ Manual	RTFM
Read the F**king Article	RTFA
Read The F**king Description	RTFD
Read The F**king Instructions	RTFI
Read The F**king Thread	RTFT
Read The FAQ	RTF
Read The Freaking FAQ	RTFF
Read The Frequently Asked Questions	RTFAQ
Read The Instructions	RTI

Read the manual stupid	RTMS
Read The Question	RTQ
Read The Silly Manual	RTSM
Read the stupid manual	RTSM
Read The Thread	RTT
Read the whole *freaking* question	RTWFQ
Read your Bible	RYB
Read Your Friendly Manual	RYFM
Read Your Screen	RYS
Real Life	RL
Real Life Conference	RLCO
Real soon now	RSN
Real Time	RT
Real World	RW
Really	RLY
Really angry and swearing	>:@
Really sad	:C
Really strong	TANK
Rear Of Convoy Covered From Police	BACK DOOR CLOSED
Reason for my happiness	RFMH
Reason to be single	RTBS
Refers to a retweet that is a shortened version of the original	CUTTWEET
Refers to 'A-list' Twitter users	TWITTERATI
Refers to the combined intelligence of all Twitter users	HIVEMIND
Refers to Twitter users who tweet excessively	TWEETERBOXES
Regarding	RE

Regards	RGS
Relaxed Bitch Face	RBF
Remember	REM
Reno NV	SIN CITY
Reply	QSL
Reply not needed	RNN
Reply not required	RNR
Request to move into the right lane	BRING YOURSELF ON IN
Request use of a busy channel	BREAK/BREAKER
Rescheduled - Change to	119
Respondez S'il Vous Plait- French for Please Reply	RSVP
Response to BYE?	BYE
Rest Area	PICKLE PARK
Rest in peace	RIP
Restaurant	325
Retention	RTNTN
Retirement	RTRMT
Retroactive	RTRCTV
Return here	107
Return on Investment	ROI
Return Receipt Request	RRQ
Retweet (Twitter slang)	RT
Right back at you	RBAY
Right F**king Now	RFN
Right Now	RN
Road Is Clear Of Police Ahead	CLEAN SHOT
Roadway Express Truck	BIG R
Robot	BOT

rocks	ROX
Roger (as in roger that/I understand)	RGR
Roger that	RT
Role Playing Game	RPG
Roll On Floor Laughing My A** Off	ROFLMAO
Roll On Floor Laughing Out Loud	ROFLOL
Roll On Mother F**king Tide	ROMFT
Roll On Tide	ROT
Roll your own	RYO
Rolling my eyes	RME
Rolling On F**king Floor Laughing	ROTFFL
Rolling On Floor Laughing	ROFL
Rolling On Floor Laughing And Screaming	ROFLAS
Rolling on floor laughing and spinning around	ROFLCOPTER
Rolling On The Floor	ROTF
Rolling on the floor but not laughing	ROFBNL
Rolling On The Floor Laughing	ROTFL
Rolling on the floor laughing at you	ROFLAY
Rolling On The Floor Laughing My A$$ Off	ROTFLMAO
Rolling On The Floor Laughing My A** Off Till I Die	ROTFLMAOTID
Rolling On The Floor Laughing My F**king A$$ Off	ROFLMFAO
Rolling On The Floor Laughing	ROTFLOL

Out Loud	
Rolling On The Floor Laughing Till I Cry	ROTFLTIC
Rolling on the floor laughing unable to speak	ROFLUTS
Rolling on the floor laughing unable to speak	ROTFLUTS
Rolling on the floor laughing with tears in my eyes	ROFLWTIME
Rolling on the floor making out	ROFMO
Rookie Cop	Baby Bear
Room	RM
Rose	---/--@
Rose	@--)--)(--
Roses to you	R2U
Run Ahead Of Others To Lure Out The Bears	Shake The Bushes
Runescape (online gaming)	RS
Running illegal station	BOOTLEGGER

S Descriptions

S**t For Brains	SFB
S**T Out of Luck	SOL
Sad	:-(
Same here	SH
Same Old Stuff	SOS
Same place same time	SPST
Same Stuff Different Day	SSDD
Same time same place	STSP
San Antonio Texas	ALAMO CITY

San Francisco CA	BAY CITY
San Francisco CA	GAY BAY
Santa	*<[:{)
Saturday	066
Save our souls	SOS
Say again	10-9
School	SKL
School/University	326
Scientific wild *a* guess	SWAG
Scratching my head in disbelief	SMHID
Screaming	:-@
Screaming With Laughter	SWL
Screwing Up Face In Disgust	SUFID
Sealed With A Kiss	SWAK
Sealed with a loving kiss	SWALK
Search F**king Google	SFG
Search Google	SG
Search the Web	STW
Secure a flatbed load	THROW SOME ROPE
See	C
See Last Mail	SLM
See Me	CME
See What I Mean	SWIM
See YA	CY
See Ya	CYA
See Ya On Return Trip	CATCH YA ON THE FLIP FLOP
See You	CU
See You All Later	CYAL8R
See you around	CUA

See you around like a donut	CURLO
See you in another life	CUIAL
See you in my dreams	CUMID
See you in the morning	SUITM
See you later	CUL
See you later	CUL8R
See you later	CYL8R
See you later	SUL
See you later	SYL
See you later alligator	CULA
See You Next Time (Originally used in Morse Code but is seldom used due to its derogatory implications)	CUNT
See you online	CYO
See you soon	324
See You Soon	CUS
See You Soon	SYS
See you tonight	195
See You Too	CU2
See you too	CUT
Sell out	7735
Send between tasks	DRIVE-BY-TWEET
Send me a Private Message	SMPM
Send me an Instant Message	SMIM
Send to receive (send me your picture to get mine)	S2R
Sender made a mistake typing their last message	MSTK
Sense of Humor	SOH
Sense of Humor Failure	SOHF

Sent (or sealed) with a kiss	SWAK
Seriously	SRSLY
Service Center/Garage	324
Set my heart on fire	SMHOF
Sexually transmitted disease	STD
Sexy	6Y
Sexy Mexican	SMEXI
Sexy or attractive	HAAT
Shaking My Damn Head	SMDH
Shaking My F**king Head	SMF
Shaking My Head	SMH
Shaking My Head Laughing	SMHL
Shaking My Mother F**king Head	SMMFH
Sharp looking rig with custom interior	BEAVER TRAP
She (Wife/Significant Other/Mother) who must be obeyed	SWMBO
Sheriff	COUNTY MOUNTY
Shifting to Neutral going downhill to Increase speed	GEORGIA OVERDRIVE
Shocked	8O
Shocked and surprised	8.O
Shopping Center	327
Short for Canada/Canadian	CAD
Short Message Service	SMS
Short of time	SOT
Short of time - must go	SOTMG
Short Time	SHORT SHORT

Should be	SB
Shrugging shoulders	MEH
Shut the *freak* up	STFU
Shut up	SH^
Shut Up	SU
Shut up and color	SUAC
Shut up and kiss me	SUAKM
Shut up you fool	SUYF
Shut Your F**king Mouth	SYFM
Shut Your Mouth	SYM
Shut your yapper	SYY
Sick	7K
Sick	CK
Sick of me yet?	SOMY
Sigh or sighing	MEHH
Significant Other	SO
Significant Other/Spouse	BETTER HALF
Single point of contact	SPOC
Sister (Mandarin Chinese)	MM
Sister for life	SFL
Sister-In-Law	SIL
Sitting In Chair Snickering	SICS
Sitting In My Chair Snickering	SIMCS
Situation normal all fouled up	SNAFU
Skate	SK8
Skater	SK8R
Skater Boy	SK8RBOI
Skating	SK8NG
Skiing/Snowboarding (This suggests a set of skis)	11
Skunk	POLE CAT
Slang term for crazy	CRA CRA

Slang term for the most beautiful of women	BUBU
Slapping head in disgust	SHID
Sleeping Hour	ZH
slim chance	10-2-1
Slow Down	Back 'em Up
Slow Down	BACK OFF THE HAMMER
Slow down	BACK'EM UP
Slow Lane	GRANNY LANE
Small child or annoying teenager	ANKLE BITER
Small Matter of Programming	SMOP
Smart a**	SA
Smart and Sexy	SMEXI
Smile	*S*
Smile	:-)
Smile	:-)
Smile	=)
Smile	S
Smiling back	SB
Smiling Ear To Ear	SETE
Smiling face	:)
Smiling Out Loud	SMOL
Smirk To Self	STS
Sneezing	:{}::
Snickering in silence	SIS
Snooze You Loose	SUL
Snot-nosed egotistical rude teenager	SNERT
Snow or Ice	GREASY

	STUFF
Snow Plow	SALT SHAKER
So Bored	SB
So F**king Bored	SFB
So F**king Funny	SFF
So F**king What	SFW
So far as I know	SFAIK
So Far So Good	SFSG
So Funny	SF
So much fun	SMF
So sorry	SS
So stupid it's funny	SSIF
So stupid it's not funny	SSINF
So The F**k What	STFW
So What	SW
Sobbing/crying (Mandarin Chinese)	555
Social Gathering	321
Social justice warrior	SJW
Social Networking Site	SNS
Someone	SOME1
Someone older you look up to	SENPAI
Someone Over Shoulder	SOS
Someone who invites their Twitter friends to interact with them on LinkedIn	TWINKEDLIN
Someone who is infatuated with another Twitter user	INTWITUATED
Someone who uses AM	ANCIENT MARINER
Someone with me	SOWM
Son of a *B*	SOAB

Sooner or later	SOL
Sorry	25
Sorry	5012124
Sorry	SRY
Sorry about that	SAT
Sorry 'bout that	SBT
Sorry for the late reply	SFLR
Sorry I could not resist	SICNR
Sorry I got to run	SIG2R
Sorry I missed your call	SIMYC
Sorry If Already Posted	SIAP
Sorry to say	S2S
Sorry! Could Not Resist!	SCNR
Sort of	SORTA
Sounds Good To Me	SGTM
Sounds like a plan	SLAP
Spam for life	S4L
Speak	SPK
Speaking Of Which	SOW
Special Agent (usually sarcasm)	SA
Speechless	....
Speeding car	BEAR BAIT
Spend The Night	STN
Split the cost as in Going Dutch	DUTCH
Spoke to	SPTO
Sponsored	SP
Sports Game	328
Square	SQ
St Louis MO	GATEWAY CITY
Stand On The Fuel Pedal	STAND ON IT

Standing back in amazement	SBIA
Stationary Police W/Radar	BEAR TRAP
Stay away for a while	616
Stay cool	SC
Stay in touch	SIT
Stay in your own lane	SIYOL
Stay Out Of My Business	SOOMB
Sticking out tongue	:-P
Sticking out tongue	SOT
Sticking tongue out	STO
Stinking up a coffin (i.e. dead)	SUAC
Stop calling me	617
Stop Playing	303
Stop texting and drive	ST&D
Stop texting and drive	ST&D
Stop that	ST
Straight	STR8
Straight or Gay?	SORG
Stressed Out Bigtime	SOB
Strike it rich	SIR
Strong CB Signal	COMIN IN LOUD & PROUD
Studying	STDNG
Stupid	S2PID
Stupid Acronyms	SA
Stupid Four Letter Acronym	SFLA
Stupid or silly	DERP
Stupidity is hard to take	SIHTH
Such a laugh	SAL
Sucks to be you	STBU
Suggested Manufacturer's	SMRP

Retail Price	
Sulfuric Acid - refers to someone with a caustic attitude	H_2SO_4
Sunday	077
Super Sweet	SS
Supermarket	310
Supposed to be	SPOZ2B
Supreme Court of the United States	SCOTUS
Surpassing All Previous Foul Ups	SAPFU
Surprised	:O
Surprised	;0
Sweet dreams	56
Sweet dreams	56
Sweet dreams	SD
Sweet dreams my baby	SDMB
Sweet young thing	SYT

T Descriptions

Take a shot	TAS
Take a walk	TAW
Take Care	TC
Take care of business	TCB
Take care of yourself	TCOY
Take my advice	TMA
Take my word for it	TMWFI
Take Over My A$$	TOMA
Take The Shot	TTS
Take your time	TURT
Take your time	TYT

Talk dirty to me	TD2M
Talk dirty to me	TDTM
Talk To You A While From Now	TTYAWFN
Talk To You Another Time	TTYAT
Talk to you awhile from now	TTYAFN
Talk to you later	TLK2UL8R
Talk to you later	TTUL
Talk to you later	TTUL8TR
Talk To You Later	TTYL
Talk To You Later If I Get A Chance	TTYLIIGAC
Talk To You Never	TTYN
Talk To You Soon	TTYS
Talk To You Tomorrow	TTYT
Talk To You Sooner Than Later	TTYSTL
Tampa FL	CIGAR CITY
Ta-Ta For Now	TTFN
Taunting a fragged/killed player (online gaming)	TBAG
Te Amo/I Love You (Spanish)	23
Te quiero/ I love you (Spanish)	TQ
Te Quiero/I Love You (Spanish)	26
Teacher in room	TIR
Tears of joy	TOJ
Tears Running Down My Cheeks	TRDMC
Teenager language only they can understand	TWEENGLISH
Tell it like it is	TILIS
Tell it to your neighbor	TTYN
Tell me I'm beautiful	TMIB
Tell Me More	TMM

Tell me please	TM{
Tell Me What It Means	TMWIM
Tell me when you arrive	QAF
Tell me your location	TMYL
Ten man (online gaming)	10M
Tender Loving Care	TLC
Tension	10sion
Terms of service	TOS
Text	TXT
Text back later	TBL
Text back later	TBL8TR
Text me back	TMB
Text me later	TML
Text the cell	TTC
Thank F**king God	TFG
Thank God	TG
Thank God it's Friday	TGIF
Thank God it's Saturday	TGIS
Thank goodness	TG
Thank you	10-400
Thank you	10Q
Thank you	1-1
Thank You	53
Thank you	TNQ
Thank you	TU
Thank You	TY
Thank you for charity (online gaming)	TYFC
Thank you for your comment	TYFYC
Thank you so much	TYSO
Thank You Very Much	TYVM
Thanks	10qs

Thanks	10X
Thanks	217
Thanks	FANKS
Thanks	THNX
Thanks	THX
Thanks	TKS
Thanks	TNX
Thanks	TX
Thanks a lot	TA
Thanks A Million	TNXE6
Thanks for being you	T4BU
Thanks for sharing	TFS
Thanks For The Follow	TFTF
Thanks For The Help Ahead Of Time	TFTHAOT
Thanks for the invitation	TFTI
Thanks for the RT (Retweet)	RTHX
Thanks For The Thought	TFTT
Thanks In Advance	TIA
Thanks So F**king Much	TSFM
Thanks So Much	TSM
Thanksgiving	TURKEY DAY
Thank-you	THNQ
That	DAT
That Is Not What I Said	TINWIS
That stinks!	PU
That was before you	TWB4U
That's All For Now	TAFN
That's	DATZ
That's a knee slapper	TAKS
That's All Folks!	TAF
That's Bull S**t	TBS

That's F**king Bull S**t	TFBS
That's For F**king Sure	TFFS
That's For Sure	TFS
That's Not What I Meant	TNWIM
That's Not What I Said	TNWIS
That's so not fair	TSNF
That's some messed up stuff	DSMUS
That's what she said	TWSS
The act of eavesdropping on other Twitter conversations	EAVESTWEETING
The act of merging Twitter and Phishing usually for unsavory reasons	TWISHING
There's A Ripple in the Force	TARITF
The act of posting on Twitter while intoxicated	DRUNKTWITTERING
The condition of being infatuated with another Twitter user	INTWITUATION
The FCC	BIG DADDY
The odds are against you	100-2-1
The Original Poster (refers to the one who started this discussion thread)	TOP
The Powers that Be	TPTB
The sender chuckles	<CHUCKLE>
The sender is frowning	<FROWN>
The sender is smiling	<SMILE>
The sender is smirking	<SMIRK>
The sender is winking	<WINK>
The sooner the better	TSTB
The State Police	BOY SCOUTS

The Twitter etiquette of acceptable behavior	TWETTIQUETTE
Theatre	317
There Ain't No Justice	TANJ
There Ain't No Such Thing As A Free Lunch	TANSTAAFL
There Ought (to) Be A Law	TOBAL
There Ought To Be A Law	TOTBAL
There's No Such Thing As A Free Lunch	TNSTAAFL
These things take time	TTTT
Things Are Really *fouled* Up	TARFU
Think Globally Act Locally	TGAL
Think happy thoughts	T:)T
Think happy thoughts	THT
Think Of Me	522
Think positive	T+
Thinking about u (you)	TAU
Thinking about you miss you always love you	TAUMUALU
Thinking of U (you)	TOU
Thinking of you	823
Thinking Of You	TOY
This	DIS
This	DIZ
This is an emergency - Call me now!	911
This Is F**king Stupid	TIFS
This is getting old	30
This Is Not A Legal Opinion	TINALO
This is odd	13579
This Is Stupid	TIS

This Ought to Be Good	TOBG
Three Finger Salute (Ctl-Alt-Del)	TFS
Throw Back Thursday	TBT
Throwing my hands up	TMHU
Thursday	044
Ticket	BLUE SLIP
Tickets	428
Till Further Notice	TFN
Till next time	TNT
Time	000
Time To Go	TTG
Tire shop	ALLIGATOR STATION
To	2
To be	2B
To Be Announced	TBA
To Be Continued	TBC
To Be Decided	TBD
To Be F**king Honest	TBFH
To Be Honest	TBH
To Be Quite F**king Honest	TBQFH
To Be Quite Honest	TBQH
To cool	2CUL
To cool for school	2C4SKOOL
To cool for you	2C4U
To die for	2D4
To drive ahead of the others and try to lure out the police	BEAT THE BUSHES
To Infinity And Beyond	TIAB
To leave a channel	BUG OUT
To Tell The Truth	TTTT

To Tell You Kindly	TTYK
To The Best Of My Knowledge	TTBOMK
To You Too	2U2
Today	288
Today	2DAY
Today I learned	TIL
Told you so	TYS
Toll Booth	CASH REGISTER
Tomorrow	2MOR
Tomorrow	2MORO
Tomorrow	2MORROW
Tomorrow	2MRW
Tomorrow a.m.	TAM
Tomorrow is another day	TIAD
Tomorrow p.m.	TPM
Tongue In Cheek	TIC
Tongue tied	:-&
Tonight	200
Tonight	2-9T
Tonight	2NTE
Too *freaking* funny	TFF
Too Bad	TB
Too cool for you	TC4U
Too cool for you	TCFU
Too cute	2CUTE
Too Damn Many	TDM
Too easy	2EZ
Too F**king Bad	TFB
Too F**king Funny	2FF
Too Fast For You	2F4U
Too Funny	2F

Too Funny	TF
Too good to be true	2G2BT
Too late	2l8
Too Late To Call	099
Too long	TL
Too long; didn't read	TL;DR
Too Much Drama	TMD
Too Much F**king Drama	TMFD
Too Much F**king Information	TMFI
Too much information	2MI
Too Much Information	TMI
Too much information (more than 411)	511
Too much to handle	2M2H
Too much to handle	TMTH
Top Gear	BIG HOLE
Total Cost of Ownership	TCO
Total F**king Nightmare	TFN
Total Nightmare	TN
Total Waste Of F**king Time	TWOFT
Total Waste Of Time	TWOT
Totally	TOTES
Totally	TTLY
Totally not funny	TNF
Totally Stinks	TS
Totally Stupid Rules	TSR
Tower defense (online gaming)	TD
Tractor Trailer or Linear Amplifier	BOX
Traffic Is Slowing Ahead - Possibly To A Stop	BRAKE CHECK
Tread parts from a blown 18	ALLIGATOR

wheeler tire left on the road	SKINS
Tripping so hard	TSH
Truck stop hooker	LOT LIZARD
Truck That Can Exceed 100 MPH	TRIPLE DIGIT RIDE
Trucker talk exchanged at truck stops eyeball-to-eyeball	BEAN HOUSE BULL
Trucker's Log Book	COMIC BOOK
Trucking Terminal	YARD
Trust me on this	TMOT
Try Before You Buy	TBYB
Trying Not To Laugh	TNTL
Trying To Keep a Straight Face	TTKSF
Tsk-Tsk	t^t
Tto tweet extremely fast	ZTWITT
Tucson AZ	BIG T
Tuesday	022
Turn a blind eye	TABE
Turn up	TURNT
Turn Your Caps Lock OFF	TOYCL
Turn Your CAPS LOCK OFF	TYCLO
Turning you in	TUI
Tweet me back	TMB
Twitter and Terrific merged used to describe something terrific found on Twitter	TWITTERIFIC
Twitter applications also called Twitter Tools or Twitter Add-Ons	TWITTERAPPS
Twitter Art	TWART
Twitter feature lets you mark a person's message as a favorite	FAV

Twitter lets you see messages from all the people you follow	FOLLOWING
Twitter terminology	TWERMINOLOGY
Twitter traffic	TWAFFIC
Twitter users	TWEEPLE
Twitterers who use Twitter to network	TWITTWORKING
Two Wheeler (motorcycle)	2W
Typical woman	X!

U Descriptions

U	U
Ugly domestic scene	UDS
Un *freaking* believable	UFB
Un de Ces Quartre/One of these days	12C4
Un/Not politically correct	UNPC
Unbelievable	:-C
Unbelievable	UNBLEFBLE
Un-Believable	UB
Uncertain	UNCRTN
Undecided	:-\
Unfortunate	UN4TUN8
Unidentified drinking injury (bruise/scratches/aches)	UDI
Universidad/University - College (Spanish)	UNI
Unmarked Police car	BROWN PAPER BAG
Unpleasant visual	UV

Unreal Tournament (online gaming)	UT
Until further notice	UFN
Until something better comes along	USBCA
Up yours	^URS
Up yours	UYRS
Upload	UL
Use F**king Google	UFG
Use Google	UG
Use no acronyms	UNA
Used to describe a fabulous tweet	TWABULOUS
Used to describe someone who is new to Twitter	TWEWBIE
Used to name another user within your tweet	MENTION
Using An Unmodified CB	BAREFOOT
Using an unmodified CB transmitter	BEARFOOT
Using services such as Twitter to update your blog	MICROBLOGG ING
Using social media microblogging to raise money	MICROFUNDI NG
Using Twitter as a form of procrastination	TWITTCRASTI NATION
Using Twitter to circulate news and information	BIRD-OF-MOUTH
Usually	USU
U-turn OR Return Trip	FLIP FLOP

V Descriptions	
Value added tax	VAT
Value for money	VFM
Very	V
Very	VRY
Very big smile	VBS
Very evil grin	VEG
Very Fast Nice Truck	LARGE CAR
Very freaking funny	VFF
Very good condition	VGC
Very good game (online gaming)	VGG
Very good hand (online gaming)	VGH
Very important person	VIP
very many thanks	VMT
Very nice	VN
Very nice hand (online gaming)	VNH
Very sad face	VSF
Very soft chuckle	VSC
Very well done (online gaming)	VWD
Very well played (online gaming)	VWP
Vice Versa	VS
Video	429
video	VID
Visible bra line	VBL
Visible panty line	VPL
Voice Mail	VM
Voice over Internet Protocol	VOIP

W Descriptions	
Wait	121
Wait	W8
Wait a minute	WAM
Wait a second	SEC
Wait a second	WAS
Walking while you Tweet using a mobile device	TWALKING
Wal-Mart	WALLY WORLD
Want to	WANNA
Want to buy (online gaming)	WTB
Want to go private (talk out of public chat area)	WTGP
Want to have Lunch?	1200
Want to hear something stupid	400
Want to play golf?	4
Want to sell? (online gaming)	WTS
Want to talk	WAN2TLK
Want to trade? (online gaming)	WTT
Want to?	WAN2
Was (alternate form)	WOZ
Wash My Mouth Out With Soap	WMMOWS
Waste Of F**king Time And Money	WOFTAM
Waste of money brains and time	WOMBAT
Waste Of Time And Money	WOTAM
Watch Your Mouth	WUM
Watch Your Mouth	WYM
Way to go	W2G
Way to Go	WTG

Way Too Much Information	WTMI
Way way to much info	WWTMI
We Are Back	WAB
We love you	243
We Owned the Other Team	W00T
Weapon (online gaming)	WEP
Webopedia	WEBO
Wednesday	033
Week	WK
Week Day	WD
Weekend	WE
Weekend	W-END
Weekend	WKD
Weekend	WKEND
Weigh Station	CHICKEN COUP
Weight Of A Truck	GROUND PRESSURE
Welcome	WC
Welcome	WLC
Welcome back	W/B
Welcome Back	WB
Well done partner	WDP
Well I'll Be A Monkey's Uncle	WIBAMU
Well known fact	WKF
West Coast	LEFT COAST
What	WUT
What (are) you doing?	WYD
What A F**king Waste Of Time	WAFWOT
What a jerk	WAJ
What A Waste Of Time	WAWOT
What About You	WAU

What about you?	WBU
What are you	WHATCHA
What Are You Doing	WRUD
What are you doing?	?RUD
What Are You Doing?	WAYD
What are you doing?	WRUD
What are you up to?	WUU2
What Did You Mean	WDYM
What did you say	WDYS
What do you know?	WDYK
What Do You Mean By That?	WDYMBT
What do you mean?	?DUM?
What Do You Think	WDYT
What do you think?	WGACA
What do you want to talk about	WDYWTTA
What goes around comes around	480
What in the world	WITW
What Is Correct Time	10-1
What is your location	10-20
What the *freak* ?	WTF
What the crap	WTC
What The F***k	WTF
What The F**k Is Your Problem?	WTFIYP
What The F**king Hell?	WTFH
What The F**king S**t	WTFS
What the heck	WTH
What the hell	WTH
What The S**t	WTS
What Time	WT
What U Want	WUW

What Would Jesus Do?	WWJD
What Would You Do?	WWYD
What you been up 2	WUBU2
What You Get Is What You Pay For	WYGISWYPF
What you see is what you get	WUCIWUG
What You See Is What You Get	WYSISWYG
What?	?
What?	W@
Whatever	15
Whatever	W/E
Whatever	WE
Whatever	WTV
Whatever Happened To	WHT
What's in it for me?	WIIFM
What's new with you	WNWU
What's the point?	WITP
What's the rush?	WTR
What's the weather forecast	QAM
What's up?	333
What's up?	SUP
What's up?	WU
What's up?	WUP
What's up?	ZUP
What's Your F**king Problem	WYFP
What's your point?	WIYP
What's Your Problem	WYP
Whatta loser	WL
When a non-celebrity Twittter user believes they are a celebrity	CELEBRITY SYNDROME
When All Else Fails	WAEF

When an individual adds all of a friend's friends to their list	FRIENDSCAPPING
When will I see you	WWICU
When you get a minute	WYGAM
When you have a minute	WYHAM
When you least expect it	WYLEI
Where (are) you from?	WUF
Where are we at?	WAWA
Where Are You	943
Where are you at?	WRU@
Where are you from?	WAYF
Where are you going	QRD
Where are you?	10-20
Where are you?	221
Where No One Has Gone Before	WNOHGB
Who are you	QRA
Who are you	WRU
Who asked you	WAU
Who cares	WC
Who cares anyway	WCA
Who died and left you in charge	WDALYIC
Who F**king Cares?	WFC
Who pulled your chain?	420
Who pulled your chain?	WPYC
Who/What/When/Where/Why	WH5
Whoop Dee Doo	WDD
Whoop Dee F**king Doo	WDFD
Who's the man?	WTM
Why	Y
Why haven't you called?	220
Why?	Y?

Wicked evil grin	WEG
Wide F**king Open	WFO
Wide Open	WO
Wife	YF
Wife over shoulder	WOS
Wi-Fi	Y5
Wild *a* guess	WAS
Wild Assed Guess	WAG
Will be late	215
will catch you later	WCUL
Will get in/Will Arrive at	122
Will wonders never cease	WWNC
Will you be on later	WUBOL
Will you call me?	WYCM
Wink	*W*
Wink	;-)
Winning is so pleasurable	WISP
Wired Telephone	LANDLINE
Wish you were here	619
Wish you were here	WYWH
With	W/
With Out Thinking	WOT
With Out Thinking Too Much	WOTTM
With Regard To	WRT
With Respect To	WRT
Without	W/O
Without Thinking	WT
Without Thinking Too Much	WTTM
Work	WRK
Work Of Art	WOA
Working at home	WAH
Works for me	WFM

World of Warcraft (online gaming)	WOW
Wouldn't It Be Nice If	WIBNI
Wouldn't That Be Nice	WTBN
Wrap it up	WIU
Write back	W/B
Write Back	WB
Write back soon	WBS
Write when you can	WWYC
Wrong way driver	NORTH BOUND HEADING SOUTH
WUZ	WUZ
WWW (Web address)	W3

Y Descriptions

Yawn	YN
Yawning	|-O
Yeah right	YR
Yeah sure you do	YSYD
Yeah yeah sure sure whatever	YYSSW
Year	YR
Years old	Y/O
Yelling Woo-Hoo out loud	YWHOL
Yes	18
Yes	YUP
Yes - Understood (now) proceed	YUP
Yes - We have no bananas	YWHNB
Yes (Russian)	DA

Yes I Understand	YIU
Yes I Will Go Private	YIWGP
Yesterday	180
Yesterday	YD
Yet another acronym	YAA
Yet Another Bloody Acronym	YABA
Yet another meeting	YAM
Yet Another Off-Topic Message	YAOTM
Yet Another Unix Nerd	YAUN
You	J00
You	U
You *freaking* with me?	UFWM
You Are	UR
You are a star	URA*
You are always in my dream	URALIMDRMS
You are always ion my mind	URAOMM
You are an angel	UAA
You Are Awesome	YAA
You Are Awesome	YRA
You are beautiful	YAB
You Are F**king Awesome	YAFA
You Are Finished	86
You got this	YGT
You are hot (U R Hot)	URH
You are not nice	UNN
You are so kind to me	URSKTM
You are the greatest!	621
You are the man	URTM
You are too wise for me	UR2WS4ME
You are welcome	URW
You Bet Your Sweet A$$	YBYSA
You Bumbling Idiot	YBI

You can have them	YCHT
You can look it up	YCLIU
You can't do business when your computer is down	YCDBWYCID
You crack me up	UCMU
You crack me up	YCMU
You did it! Bravo!	430
You don't know	UDK
You don't know	YDK
You F**king Idiot	UFI
You F**king Idiot	YFI
You forgot	109
You Get The Idea?	YGTI
You Get What You Pay For	YGWYPF
You go girl	YGG
You have been trolled	YHBT
You have been warned	YHBW
You have got to be s#$t*ing me!	UHGTBSM
You have lost	YHL
You Idiot	UI
You know	UNO
You know that's right	UKTR
You know what	YKW
You Know What I Mean	YKWIM
You know what you can do	YKWYCD
You Know Your Addicted To ...	YKYAT
You Know You're A Redneck When	YKYARW
You made my day	YMMD
You never know	YNK
You Only Live Once	YOLO

You Owe Me	UOM
You Owe Me	YOM
You owe me big time	1040
You owe me big time	410
You Owe Me Big Time	UOMBT
You rock	URK
You slay me	USM
You Snooze You Loose	YSUL
You Suck	29
You take too long	UT2L
You take too long	YTTL
You tell me	UTM
You the man!	1
You the one!	1
You there?	YT
You Too	U2
You will	UW
You win some - you lose some	YWSYLS
You Wish	135
You with the long face	UWTLF
You'd	UD
You-Da-Man	UDM
You'll	ULL
You'll be sorry	YBS
Young gentleman	YG
Young Lady	YL
Young Man	YM
Your	J00R
Your	YR
Your Brother From Another Mother	YBFAM
Your brother in Christ	YBIC

Your comment to?	YCT
Your cool	36
Your F**king Problem	YFP
Your Home	HOME 20
Your mileage may vary	YMMV
Your most welcome	YMW
Your not the boss	YNTB
Your own boss	YOB
Your perfect	10
Your Problem	YP
Your quite welcome	YQW
Your revolting	1776
Your sister in Christ	YSIC
Your way out there	2001
Your/You're (You Are)	UR
You're Dead	187
You're finished	86
You're Gonna Love It	YGLI
You're Gonna Love This	YGLT
You're in loony land	490
You're in trouble buddy	420
You're late (Read upside down)	87
I'm late (Read upside down)	87
You're On Your Own	YOYO
You're perfect	10
You're revolting	1776
You're running your own cuckoo clock	YRYOCC
You're terrific	2468
You're the best	YTB
You're the greatest	YTG
You're the one; you da man!	1

You're too kind	Y2K
You're very welcome	YVW
You're way out there	2001
You're welcome	YW
Yourself	URSELF
You've Got To Be Kidding	YGTBK
You've got to be Kidding me	YGTBKM

Z Descriptions

Zero	Z
Zero hand (online gaming)	19
Zero tolerance	ZOT
Zoo	Z%

About the Author

Mitch Sexton is a pseudonym used by Evans Bissonette to make it easier for both his non-fiction and his fiction readers to identify books in the respective genres.

In addition to *WTF r u sayin'?*, Mitch Sexton wrote Pick-3 Lottery Tips and Strategies.

In the (action adventure) arena, Evans Bissonette, wrote The Ice Age Saga Trilogy—*The Shaman's Song, The Sojourner's Tale*, and *Crooked Foot*.

In addition to the above, he wrote a historical fiction *Explorer!*

All are written as action-adventure stories meant to entertain readers of all ages.

The author and his wife, both retired, have been married 46 years. They live in a suburb of Detroit and have three adult children of whom they are very proud.